ASEAN Centrality and the ASEAN-US Economic Relationship

About the East-West Center

The East-West Center promotes better relations and understanding among the people and nations of the United States, Asia, and the Pacific through cooperative study, research, and dialogue. Established by the US Congress in 1960, the Center serves as a resource for information and analysis on critical issues of common concern, bringing people together to exchange views, build expertise, and develop policy options.

The Center's 21-acre Honolulu campus, adjacent to the University of Hawai'i at Mānoa, is located midway between Asia and the US mainland and features research, residential, and international conference facilities. The Center's Washington, DC, office focuses on preparing the United States for an era of growing Asia Pacific prominence.

The Center is an independent, public, nonprofit organization with funding from the US government, and additional support provided by private agencies, individuals, foundations, corporations, and governments in the region.

Policy Studies
an East-West Center series

Series Editors
Edward Aspinall and Dieter Ernst

Description
Policy Studies presents scholarly analysis of key contemporary domestic and international political, economic, and strategic issues affecting Asia in a policy relevant manner. Written for the policy community, academics, journalists, and the informed public, the peer-reviewed publications in this series provide new policy insights and perspectives based on extensive fieldwork and rigorous scholarship.

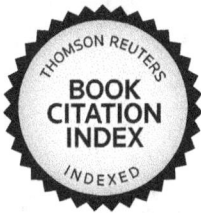

THOMSON REUTERS
BOOK CITATION INDEX
INDEXED

The East-West Center is pleased to announce that the Policy Studies series has been accepted for indexing in Web of Science Book Citation Index. The Web of Science is the largest and most comprehensive citation index available.

Notes to Contributors
Submissions may take the form of a proposal or complete manuscript. For more information on the Policy Studies series, please contact the Series Editors.

Editors, Policy Studies
East-West Center
1601 East-West Road
Honolulu, Hawai'i 96848-1601
Tel: 808.944.7197
Publications@EastWestCenter.org
EastWestCenter.org/PolicyStudies

Policy
Studies | 69

ASEAN Centrality and the ASEAN-US Economic Relationship

Peter A. Petri and Michael G. Plummer

ASEAN Centrality and the ASEAN-US Economic Relationship
Peter A. Petri and Michael G. Plummer

ISSN 1547-1349 (print) and 1547-1330 (electronic)
ISBN 978-0-86638-246-5 (print) and 978-0-86638-247-2 (electronic)

Hard copies of all titles, and free electronic copies of most titles, are available from:

Publication Sales Office
East-West Center
1601 East-West Road
Honolulu, Hawai'i 96848-1601
Tel: 808.944.7145
Fax: 808.944.7376
EWCBooks@EastWestCenter.org
EastWestCenter.org/PolicyStudies

In Asia, hard copies of all titles, and electronic copies of select Southeast Asia titles, co-published in Singapore, are available from:

Institute of Southeast Asian Studies
30 Heng Mui Keng Terrace
Pasir Panjang Road, Singapore 119614
publish@iseas.edu.sg
bookshop.iseas.edu.sg

Contents

List of Acronyms

ADMM+8	ASEAN Defense Ministers' Meeting Plus Eight
ADVANCE	ASEAN Development Vision to Advance National Cooperation and Economic Integration
AEC	ASEAN Economic Community
AFAS	ASEAN Framework Agreement on Services
AFTA	ASEAN Free Trade Area
APEC	Asia-Pacific Economic Cooperation
ARF	ASEAN Regional Forum
ASEAN	Association of Southeast Asian Nations
APT	ASEAN Preferential Trade Agreement
BTA	US-Vietnam Bilateral Trade Agreement
CEPII	Centre d'Etudes Prospectives et d'Informations Internationales
CGE	computable general equilibrium
CIJK	FTAs among China, India, Japan, and South Korea
CJK	agreement among China, Japan, and South Korea

CLMV	Cambodia, Lao PDR, Myanmar, and Vietnam
E3	Expanded Economic Engagement initiative
EAI	Enterprise for ASEAN Initiative
EAS	East Asian Summit
EU	European Union
FDI	foreign direct investment
f.o.b.	free on board
FTA	free trade area
FTAAP	Free Trade Agreement Asia Pacific
FTAAPX	Free Trade Area of the Asia Pacific plus India
GATT	General Agreement on Tariffs and Trade
GDP	gross domestic product
IT	information technology
NTBs	nontariff barriers to trade
P4	Trans-Pacific Strategic Economic Partnership agreement
RCEP	Regional Comprehensive Economic Partnership
SEATO	Southeast Asia Treaty Organization
STAR	Support for Trade Acceleration project
TAC	Treaty of Amity and Cooperation in Southeast Asia
TIFAs	Trade and Investment Framework Arrangements
TPP	Trans-Pacific Partnership
WTO	World Trade Organization

Executive Summary

ASEAN has become a focal point of the rapidly changing economic architecture of the Asia-Pacific region. ASEAN members are increasingly stable and politically confident, and constitute an emerging economic powerhouse. The region is dynamic, with 600 million citizens and a gross domestic product (GDP) that exceeds $2 trillion and is expected to grow 6 percent annually for the next two decades. (The Appendix at the end of this paper reports detailed output and trade projections to 2025.) Through deeper internal integration via the ASEAN Economic Community (AEC) and external initiatives such as the Regional Comprehensive Economic Partnership (RCEP), ASEAN is becoming a driving force in regional cooperation and a much-courted economic partner. The AEC and the RCEP projects are globally significant: the AEC could generate powerful demonstration effects for other developing regions, and the RCEP could become an important building bloc of the multilateral trading system.

ASEAN is a dynamic regional economy of $2 trillion and a driving force in regional cooperation

"ASEAN centrality," a relatively new term, has emerged as useful shorthand for a wide range of Southeast Asian efforts to advance regional cohesion, economic integration, and international influence. ASEAN centrality is often seen as a tool and benchmark for both promoting regional integration initiatives and shaping external relationships with partners such as the United States. Centrality is desirable not only for the region, but also for most external partners—a vibrant, integrated ASEAN makes a stronger economic partner and a more reliable political ally.

Can the United States deepen its engagement with ASEAN, while also respecting the region's quest for centrality? ASEAN is a key strategic and economic partner of the United States, and its importance is projected to rise over time. ASEAN is an attractive destination for US exports and outward foreign direct investment (FDI)—for example, US investments in Singapore alone are twice those in China. But the United States has resisted an ASEAN-wide free trade area (FTA) based on relatively weak rules acceptable to all ASEAN members. In turn, US efforts to develop rigorous relationships with selected ASEAN countries have been criticized as disrupting regional cooperation. Some welcome the American presence as a guarantor of regional security, but still prefer to leave economic policy to ASEAN decision makers alone.

ASEAN and its partners, including the United States, face critical decisions that bear on ASEAN centrality. These include trade negotiations in the RCEP and the Trans-Pacific Partnership (TPP), which currently excludes most ASEAN members. How should ASEAN and the United States approach these projects?

Economics argues for a nuanced approach. Elements of centrality that contribute to greater integration and better terms in agreements with external partners will certainly benefit the region. But economic integration has not yet advanced to a level that would enable the region to act as a single unit. Limiting external economic relationships to common agreements is not yet desirable, since that would constrain the ability of members to pursue what may be very different types of gains from trade and investment. For globally competitive economies like Singapore, regional markets are not big enough, and ASEAN-style agreements are not deep enough to ensure sufficient market access. For less advanced ASEAN economies, in turn, Singapore-style liberalization may be politically unachievable. At the same time, middle-ground agreements are not likely to satisfy anyone.

ASEAN centrality can be reconciled with the region's diverse economic interests through a two-speed strategy. On one hand, members will want to maximize their individual—and consequently the region's —economic potential through close ties with external partners.

On the other hand, they will need to intensify integration within ASEAN and support less advanced members in becoming more competitive in the global marketplace.

From the viewpoint of the United States, the two-speed approach argues for welcoming ASEAN members into the TPP if they are ready to assume rigorous obligations, while joining ASEAN as a unit in policies that support capacity building, connectivity, and reform. This latter point is particularly important; as more ASEAN members join the TPP, the potential for negative economic effects on excluded members rises. The two-speed strategy

> *ASEAN centrality can be promoted through strong ties with external partners as well as deeper ASEAN integration*

has solid underpinnings in the Kemp-Wan theorem on trade agreements, which shows that regional cooperation can be applied to the benefit of all if complemented with policies that extend gains across the region.

Using novel computable general equilibrium (CGE) modeling approaches, the gains from ASEAN centrality, the RCEP, and the TPP are found to be considerable. Completing the AEC will increase regional GDP by over 5 percent, with all member countries registering gains. The RCEP and the TPP, and other wider external agreements, could contribute significant additional gains.

The TPP, in particular, would generate large benefits for ASEAN as a whole, especially if it were expanded from the current four negotiators (Brunei, Malaysia, Singapore, and Vietnam) to include also Indonesia, the Philippines, and Thailand. ASEAN's total gains are estimated to be three times as great with the TPP as under the RCEP, since the TPP provides for deeper integration and preferential access to large new markets, while the RCEP overlaps an already complete network of FTAs between ASEAN and other members.

ASEAN policymakers should not be misled by the argument that they must choose between the RCEP and the TPP, since both produce gains. Moreover, these benefits are complementary—the TPP focuses on deeper integration with the Americas, and the RCEP on continuing integration across Asian markets. This report finds that the benefits of implementing both agreements simultaneously amount to roughly 90 percent of the sum of benefits derived from implementing each agreement alone—in other words, the agreements deliver different, largely complementary gains. At the same time, overlapping membership between the two initiatives should ensure that they do not devolve into competing blocs.

Finally, the TPP itself can be designed to support the goals of ASEAN centrality. The partnership can include provisions accessible to all reform-minded economies, and focus on competition and economic efficiency rather than rules prescribing specific governance or business systems. It can create an accession clause that makes it easy for new economies to join, identify future accession windows, and offer mechanisms for bridging the RCEP and the TPP. Furthermore, the TPP can be accompanied, as argued below, by measures that extend its benefits to all ASEAN member states.

These new integration efforts, in turn, could play an important role in helping shape the global trading system. Just as ASEAN faces a false choice between the TPP and RCEP, the global trading system faces a false choice between multilateralism and regionalism, as the latter process in Asia could easily support the former if fashioned correctly. At the World Trade Organization's (WTO) Ninth Ministerial Meeting in Bali in December 2013, members succeeded in delivering the first important liberalization

Just as ASEAN faces a false choice between the TPP and RCEP, so does the global trading system between multilateralism and regionalism

package since the launch of the Doha Development Agenda in 2001, including agreements pertinent to trade facilitation, agriculture, and development-related issues. These are all areas being taken up in the TPP and, most likely, the RCEP, and the results may serve to guide multilateral progress in these and other key sectors in the future. The WTO leaders should not consider regionalism in the Asia-Pacific region as a threat, but rather as an opportunity.

ASEAN Centrality and the ASEAN-US Economic Relationship

The Challenge of the ASEAN-US Relationship

As the United States deepens its engagement with Asia, the ten countries of the Association of Southeast Asian Nations (ASEAN) are prominent on its policy horizon. The region has a dynamic economy with nearly 600 million people, lies at the crossroads of huge markets, straddles critical shipping lanes, and controls substantial agricultural, mineral, and energy resources. It is both strategically and economically significant.

Meanwhile, ASEAN members are increasingly stable and politically confident, and they are stepping up their geopolitical role by promoting "ASEAN centrality" in regional and global decisions. This new, widely used, yet ambiguous term roughly calls for the coordination of member decisions to further common interests.[1] It is often seen also as a benchmark for the region's external relationships, especially with partners such as the United States. Centrality is implicit, for example, in the recommendation that the United States "adopt a more pluralist approach

> *ASEAN members are stepping up their geopolitical role by promoting 'ASEAN centrality' in regional and global decisions*

that moves beyond an old bilateralism in acknowledgment of new actors and changing regional dynamics" (Ba 2009).

Can the United States deepen its engagement with ASEAN, while also respecting the region's quest for centrality?[2] The United States has resisted ASEAN-wide economic agreements, such as those the region has with other partners, given that they would have to be based on weak rules acceptable to all ASEAN members. In turn, US efforts to develop rigorous relationships with selected ASEAN partners have been criticized as disrupting regional cooperation. For example, a recent article in the *Jakarta Post* argued that "history teaches us that the reasons behind the absence of solid Asian regionalism and identity derive not only from domestic problems and interstate distrust among Asian countries, but also from the presence of external powers like the US in the region...ASEAN should not let the Americans re-establish their own domination in the region" (Fitriani 2010). Others welcome American presence as a guarantor of regional security, but would prefer to leave economic policy to ASEAN decision makers.

In short, US engagement with ASEAN faces controversy and suspicion. Asian concerns are diverse and have complex historical, political, and cultural roots. They will not be resolved by economic arguments alone. Nevertheless, economic logic can inform critical decisions that ASEAN, the United States, and other Asia-Pacific countries now have to make. The large trade agreements being considered in the region—the Regional Comprehensive Economic Partnership (RCEP) negotiations and the Trans-Pacific Partnership (TPP) negotiations—pose especially important choices.[3] How should ASEAN and the United States approach these projects? Is there a need to choose between them?

To understand the economics of these decisions, the paper examines the logic of the centrality argument in some detail, and draws on recent quantitative studies of alternative trade policies conducted by Fan Zhai and the authors (Petri, Plummer, and Zhai 2012a; Petri, Plummer, and Zhai 2012b). These results, along with related economic theory, are used to demonstrate the value of ASEAN centrality to the region, as well as to other partners; to examine the region's options regarding the TPP and the RCEP initiatives; and to develop guidelines for the expanding economic relationship between ASEAN and the United States.

The results confirm the value of external trade agreements to ASEAN. They also highlight the benefits of joining the TPP, since that agreement would improve access to markets not so far covered by ASEAN trade agreements. Ultimately, the paper argues for a two-speed framework for implementing centrality in the ASEAN-US context. On one level, noting ASEAN's diverse membership, it argues that several members, and so potentially the region as a whole, would benefit from ambitious, productive partnerships with the United States and other countries outside the region. On another level, noting that regional solidarity also adds value to the region and its partners, the paper also suggests parallel policies by ASEAN and external partners to promote reform and international competitiveness in less advanced ASEAN economies.

While based on novel quantitative results and theoretical arguments, these recommendations, in fact, support policies that the United States (and for that matter other ASEAN partners such as China and Japan) have more or less followed in Southeast Asia. This paper offers a fuller rationale for two-speed cooperation and offers specific examples of how ASEAN can increase its income through external partnerships, and deepen its own regional ties. The rationale is built on the well-known Kemp-Wan (1976) theorem on optimal regional cooperation, which shows that even discriminatory partnerships, such as the TPP, can benefit countries that are *not* part of the agreement, provided that they are appropriately structured. The two-speed approach suggests more freedom for extra-ASEAN relationships than many writers advocate, but also more emphasis on the intra-ASEAN obligations of members (and their external partners) that benefit from external agreements.

The two-speed approach suggests more freedom for extra-ASEAN relationships, but also more emphasis on the intra-ASEAN obligations of members

In today's setting, the framework justifies the participation of Brunei, Malaysia, Singapore, and Vietnam in the Trans-Pacific Partnership. Indeed, it suggests that other ASEAN economies—in particular, Indonesia, the Philippines, and Thailand—will face large economic incentives to join once the TPP becomes reality. Thus, all of ASEAN's largest economies could become members, further helping to reinforce their regional commitments in the ASEAN Economic Community (AEC) and elsewhere. The two-speed framework also envisions parallel ASEAN-wide initiatives, such as the recently launched US Expanded Economic Engagement (E3) initiative, as well as even more ambitious programs to promote ASEAN connectivity. In effect, advanced ASEAN members and outside partners would maximize benefits from closer trade relations, while jointly establishing mechanisms to prepare all ASEAN members to operate under similar rules. These mechanisms would help to connect less advanced countries to global supply chains—perhaps indirectly at first through members with stronger external linkages—and also support them in capacity building and reform.

The paper is organized as follows: Section II examines the quantitative details of the significance of the ASEAN-US economic relationship (more detail on future prospects is considered in the Appendix). Section III explores the concept of ASEAN centrality and its implications for intraregional and extra-regional cooperation. Section IV examines how ASEAN has, in reality, practiced intraregional and extra-regional integration. Section V focuses on possible choices between the RCEP and the TPP initiatives. Section VI returns to the policy implications for the ASEAN–United States relationship, providing details on the propositions introduced in this section. Section VII concludes.

ASEAN's Strategic and Economic Significance

Why is ASEAN important globally, and especially to the United States? First, the region is strategically significant, not least because the transport links that connect Asia and the Middle East and Europe pass through its narrow waterways. It is also a potential flashpoint from a security perspective *inter alia* due to conflicting national claims to the South China Sea. Yet despite its fragile setting, Southeast Asia has a remarkable history of resisting outside domination, and it has carefully navigated its way among the large powers of Asia and the West. The region's independence today is, in fact, an important global public good.

Second, ASEAN is an emerging economic powerhouse. Its GDP exceeds \$2 trillion (3 percent of world GDP) and is likely to grow at an average rate of 6 percent per annum for the next two decades (see the Appendix for long-term projections of ASEAN growth). Its unusually open economies are important in global supply chains. As Table 1 shows, ASEAN's trade/GDP ratio is a high 135 percent, and its foreign direct investment (FDI) stocks amount to 52 percent of GDP, compared to 17 percent for the United States. Despite the Asian financial crisis of 1997–98 and the global financial crisis in 2008–2009, FDI inflows rebounded to a record $111 billion in 2012, greatly exceeding flows into India and closing in on those into China (Table 2).

These factors have made ASEAN a sought-after partner in both security and trade initiatives. With respect to trade, ASEAN has completed many free trade areas (FTAs) with Asian partners, starting with a pathbreaking initiative with China in 2003, and it is now attempting to knit these together under the RCEP. More recently, four ASEAN economies joined 12 countries from around the Pacific to negotiate the TPP. Both projects have critics: some see the RCEP as too slow and too weak to make a difference, while others consider the TPP too intrusive for countries in the early stages of development.

> *ASEAN is an emerging economic powerhouse and a sought-after partner in both security and trade initiatives*

Table 1 further illustrates the region's diversity and the fundamental challenge this poses to ASEAN integration efforts. Singapore's per capita income is 50 times that of Cambodia, and Indonesia has 500 times as many people as Brunei. Barriers to business and trade are among the world's lowest in Singapore, Malaysia, and Thailand, but remain high in other countries, including large ones such as Indonesia and the Philippines. These differences are an obstacle to common, high-quality trade rules. An agreement that includes all ASEAN countries is likely to have watered-down rules, while an agreement with rigorous standards is likely to exclude some members.

At the same time, the region is rapidly becoming more integrated with its neighbors and the global economy, and its trade is becoming more sophisticated. In the last two decades, ASEAN trade has shifted in destination and composition from natural resource–intensive goods to electronics and other relatively sophisticated manufactures

Table 1. The ASEAN Economy, 2011

	United States	ASEAN	Brunei	Cambodia	Indonesia	Lao PDR	Malaysia	Myanmar	Philippines	Singapore	Thailand	Vietnam
Macroeconomic indicators												
Population (mill)	312	598	0.4	14	242	6	29	48	95	5	70	88
GDP ($bill)	14,991	2,151	16	13	847	8	288	45	225	240	346	124
GDP per capita ($)	48,112	3,598	40,301	897	3,495	1,320	9,977	939	2,370	46,241	4,972	1,407
Trade/GDP (%)	32	135	111	153	51	66	170	44	62	425	158	181
Inward FDI stock/GDP (%)	17	52	4	16	22	13	40	5	11	258	42	19
Growth rates 2005–2011												
GDP (%)	0.9	5.5	0.9	6.7	5.9	8.0	4.5	8.5	4.8	6.2	3.0	6.8
Exports (%)	5.3	5.8	-1.8	11.9	7.4	9.8	2.5	NA	3.8	6.1	5.2	7.0
Imports (%)	1.3	6.3	6.3	11.7	6.7	7.0	3.9	NA	3.2	5.7	4.1	8.1
Foreign Direct Investment												
Outward stock ($bill)	4,156	451	4	0	8	0	106	1	4	319	8	1
Inward stock ($bill)	2,548	1,119	1	2	186	1	115	2	26	618	146	24
From US	–	108	0	0	10	0	12	0	4	68	13	1

Table 1. The ASEAN Economy, 2011 (continued)

	United States	ASEAN	Brunei	Cambodia	Indonesia	Lao PDR	Malaysia	Myanmar	Philippines	Singapore	Thailand	Vietnam
Trade												
Exports of goods ($mill)	1,480	1,237	12	7	201	2	228	9	48	410	223	97
Exports of services ($mill)	589	255	1	2	20	1	36	1	15	129	41	9
Imports of goods ($mill)	2,266	1,152	3	9	176	2	187	9	64	366	229	107
Imports of services ($mill)	395	264	2	1	32	0	38	1	12	114	52	12
Protection												
Agricultural most favored nation (MFN) tariffs (%)	5.0	11.0	0.1	15.2	8.1	19.5	10.8	8.7	8.7	0.2	220	17.0
Nonagricultural MFN tariffs (%)	3.3	6.2	2.9	10.3	6.9	8.2	5.8	5.1	5.7	0.0	8.0	8.7
Duties collected/Imports (%)	1.2	2.2		3.9	2.1	4.6	1.0			0.0	1.4	
GATT service commitments (n)	110	62	22	94	45	79	73	5	51	67	75	105
Doing Business rank	4			141	130	166	14	NA	136	1	17	99

Note: Figures in italics are compiled from data reported by partner countries.
Sources: World Trade Organization profiles accessed August 3, 2013, http://stat.wto.org/CountryProfile/WSDBCountryPFHome.aspx?Language=E; International Monetary Fund Coordinated Direct Investment Survey, accessed June 22, 2013, http://cdis.imf.org/.

Table 2. FDI Inflows to ASEAN Economies, China, and India, Selected Years, 1995–2012
(US$ million)

	1995	2000	2005	2008	2010	2012
Brunei	583	550	289	330	626	850
Cambodia	151	149	381	815	783	1,557
Indonesia	4,419	-4,550	8,336	9,318	13,771	19,853
Lao PDR	95	34	28	227	279	294
Malaysia	5,815	3,788	4,065	7,172	9,060	10,074
Myanmar	318	208	235	863	1,285	2,243
Philippines	1,459	2,240	1,854	1,544	1,298	2,797
Singapore	11,943	15,515	18,090	12,200	53,623	56,651
Thailand	2,070	3,410	8,067	8,455	9,147	8,607
Vietnam	1,780	1,298	1,954	9,579	8,000	8,368
ASEAN TOTAL	28,632	22,641	43,299	50,504	97,870	111,294
China	37,521	40,715	72,406	108,312	114,734	121,080
India	2,151	3,588	7,622	47,139	21,125	25,542

Source: ASEAN Secretariat, *ASEAN Foreign Direct Investment Statistics Database;* UNCTAD, *World Investment Report Annex Tables.*

Figure 1. ASEAN Trade Patterns, 2001 and 2011

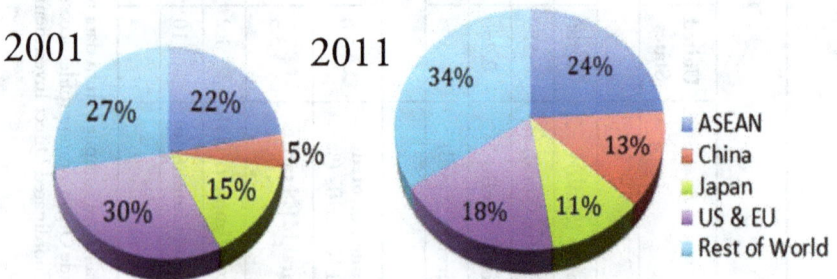

Source: United Nations Commodity Trade Statistics Database (UN Comtrade).

Figure 2. ASEAN's Share of Total US Exports and Imports by Sector, 2010

US exports (ASEAN's % of total)   US imports (ASEAN's % of total)

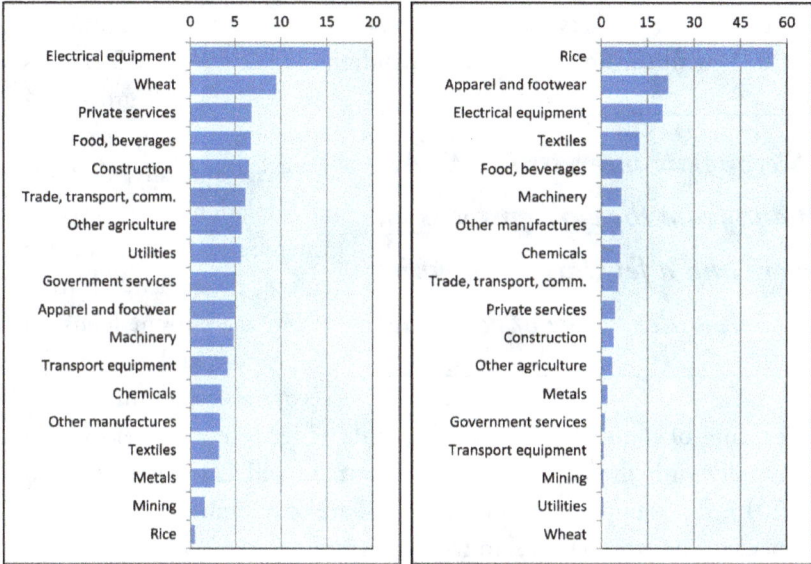

Source: Authors' model simulations, as described in Petri, Plummer, and Zhai 2012b.

embedded in global supply chains. Economic ties with the rest of emerging Asia have intensified: China's share of ASEAN trade has almost tripled from 5 percent in 2001 to 13 percent in 2011, while the US and European Union (EU) share has nearly halved, from 30 percent to 18 percent (Figure 1). And manufactured exports now account for three-fourths of ASEAN exports, ranging from low-wage products in Cambodia and Vietnam to advanced electronics in Malaysia. Thermionic valves, for example, accounted for 16 percent of total ASEAN exports and captured one-third of world markets.[4]

ASEAN is a major US trade partner in several important products (Figure 2). It was the destination for 15 percent of US electrical equipment exports (five times the region's share of world GDP), which was used in supply chains across Singapore, the Philippines, Thailand, and other countries. US exports also included raw materials—wheat and food products—and many services. On the import side, ASEAN supplied much of US rice imports, as well as significant shares of apparel and footwear (Vietnam is the second largest supplier behind China), electrical equipment, and other manufactures.

The prospects for ASEAN-US economic relations, set out in detail in the Appendix, are also strong. The analysis demonstrates that (1) ASEAN markets are likely to grow by 6 percent per annum until 2025, with consumer demand expanding even faster; (2) US exports to ASEAN will grow at 4 percent and imports at 3 percent annually; and (3) US relations with ASEAN members will become more diversified, shifting from the current focus on Singapore and a few large economies to a much wider range of countries. In particular, trade with Myanmar is set to grow rapidly with the removal of punitive trade and FDI restrictions in 2013; for example, in 2000, the US share of Myanmar's trade was 9 percent, but this fell to zero with the sanctions.[5]

> *US economic interests in ASEAN will expand from the current focus on Singapore and a few large economies to a much wider range of countries*

ASEAN Centrality

Cooperation among ASEAN countries—following on the heels of serious conflicts among them—has already paid high dividends by generating political stability. Stability, in turn, has provided a platform for economic development and productive engagement with larger powers outside the region. This section demonstrates that the same chain of causation, now associated with the pursuit of centrality, can continue to benefit the region and its external partners.

The accomplishments of recent decades would have seemed fanciful at ASEAN's launch in 1967. In retrospect, the results were a product of patient, skillful political and economic management. Appropriately, policymakers attach a high priority to pragmatism and regional solidarity, as reflected in many regional initiatives and institutions, as well as in the centrality concept itself. Centrality is hard to pin down and has been viewed skeptically by many scholars (Ravenhill 2009). Yet the concept of centrality, and more fundamentally that of intra-ASEAN regional cooperation, encompasses activities that have significant value to ASEAN and its external partners.

ASEAN began as a political organization to ward off the threat of the 1960s insurgencies. As the war in Vietnam and later Cambodia wound down in the 1970s and 1980s, attention was turned to region building through security initiatives, such as the ASEAN Regional Forum (ARF), and eventually through economics, especially with the ASEAN Free Trade Area (AFTA) in the early 1990s. Foreign investments were welcomed and regional supply chains were established by firms from advanced economies, including Japan and the United States. ASEAN also initiated "constructive engagement" to bring former adversaries on board, including Vietnam in 1995, Lao PDR and Myanmar in 1997, and Cambodia in 1999.[6] Integration continues on both the political and economic tracks through initiatives such as the ASEAN Charter and its economic pillar, the ASEAN Economic Community (AEC).

This trajectory has increased confidence in ASEAN. In turn, a sense of common identity has also begun to develop, with surveys indicating that people from several countries increasingly view themselves as citizens of ASEAN, not just their own countries (Thompson and Chulanee, 2008). The imperative to integrate ASEAN economies has been reinforced by competitive pressure from China and India, each of which offers greater economies of scale than the Southeast Asia region as a whole.

ASEAN centrality is, in effect, shorthand for regional integration and for the leverage that this might bring to the region's international linkages. It is both a goal—the vision of integrated member states—and potentially a formula for achieving it, such as the prescription that members coordinate policies. This section examines the concept in detail, in part to draw out implications for relationships with the United States and other external partners.

An Anatomy of Centrality

What exactly does centrality require from ASEAN members and partners? Concrete definitions are scarce. The earliest uses of the term refer to ASEAN cooperation on extra-group issues. However, the extent of cooperation—say, whether external agreements should be jointly concluded, or centrally overseen, or negotiated in consultation with other members—has never been specified. And rather than making the concept more precise, recent usage has ranged more broadly, covering intraregional policy decisions and the leadership of pan-Asian economic and political architectures. In this last sense, centrality even appears to apply to ASEAN's role in Asia rather than in Southeast Asia itself.

Predecessors of the centrality concept (Jones 2010) can be found in the plans for ARF, the security dialogue formed in 1994 to foster consultation on security and preventive diplomacy.[7] A concept paper published in 1995 identified ASEAN as "the primary driving force of the ARF," leading to the now widely used formulation that ASEAN occupies "the driver's seat" of regional cooperation. This intriguing, ambiguous idea has attracted much commentary and some mirth (Humaidah 2012): a driver can set directions, or follow instructions from passengers, or take intermediate courses between these extremes.

The ASEAN Charter tried to make things clearer. Article I committed "to maintain the centrality and proactive role of ASEAN as the primary driving force in its relations and cooperation with its external partners in a regional architecture that is open, transparent, and inclusive." This is an externally oriented definition, and the charter later confirms that "the strategic policy directions of ASEAN's external relations shall be set by the ASEAN Summit upon the recommendations of the ASEAN Foreign Ministers Meeting."

Following in these steps, the ASEAN Economic Community Blueprint noted that "ASEAN shall work towards maintaining 'ASEAN Centrality' in its external economic relations, including, but not limited to, its negotiations for free trade (FTAs) and Comprehensive Economic Partnerships (CEPs) agreements." But it set weak guidelines for cooperation, calling merely for "a system for enhanced coordination, and possibly arriving at common approaches and/or positions in ASEAN's external economic relations" (ASEAN 2007). In practice, ASEAN FTAs have been collections of bilateral agreements between members and external partners (Hiratsuka, Isono, Sato, and Umezaki 2008).

Subsequent documents made centrality more ambitious, but not more specific. For example, centrality has been described as a goal for coordinated decision making on intra-ASEAN policies (akin to the role of the European Commission in intra-European regulations). Former Secretary General Surin Pitsuwan has argued that ASEAN has to work on becoming a "center of growth, center of gravity, fulcrum of emerging regional architectures, new growth area, and landscape." He noted that centrality has external and internal dimensions, and requires members "to stay united, increase coordination, and participate as a cohesive group with clear common objectives" (Pitsuwan 2009).

Other references have emphasized ASEAN's potential role in the community of Asian nations. The *Roadmap for the ASEAN Community* suggests that beyond coordinating the external policies of members, ASEAN should become "the driving force in charting the evolving regional architecture" (ASEAN 2009). The *Roadmap* often uses the concepts of centrality, driving force, and shaping regional architecture side by side. A driving force in this sense is far more than a driver—it sets directions, engineers compromises, and provides leadership.

The RCEP is arguably the most concrete and ambitious example of centrality in the economic sphere. But ASEAN's role as a pan-Asian leader will ultimately depend on the successful completion of the AEC. There has been progress on the AEC, but the project is not likely to meet its timetable (Asian Development Bank 2013). For international credibility, the region will have to demonstrate its ability to create common markets and to function as an integrated economy entity (Petri and Vo 2012).

> *ASEAN's role as a pan-Asian leader will ultimately depend on the successful completion of the AEC*

How Centrality Affects ASEAN

If centrality brings deeper intraregional integration, it should produce large economic benefits for ASEAN. It can be expected to generate increased specialization and higher productivity, freer capital and labor flows, greater competition, and less rent seeking. Section IV assigns magnitudes to these effects, based on results from simulation studies.

As importantly, regional integration will attract FDI inflows. ASEAN will be more profitable as an integrated economic space than as ten separate countries, each with a small fraction of the region's 600 million people. FDI will also benefit by locking in liberal policies. And as production clusters gain traction, the region's advantages will increase, helping to create ASEAN supply chains that collaborate and compete with those in China and India.

Common positions on international agreements, however, will not necessarily generate such ambitious results. They would perhaps enable ASEAN members to achieve better terms in external negotiations, but they would also impede decisions that will be seen as important to some members. For globally competitive economies like Singapore, regional markets will not be big enough, and ASEAN-style agreements with outside partners will not produce sufficient market access abroad. For less advanced ASEAN economies, in contrast, rapid liberalization may conflict with development objectives. At the same time, middle-ground regional agreements are unlikely to satisfy anyone.

In practice, many member countries already see common external positions as unnecessary constraints. They are tempted to bypass ASEAN to forge deeper ties with outsiders and each other, in effect sacrificing leverage from concerted action for the benefits of ambitious independence (Atje 2008). As already noted, even ASEAN-Plus-One agreements have been forced, in practice, to adopt terms that vary across member-states. The difficulty of reconciling interests may be a reason why ASEAN documents avoid defining centrality, or prescribing mechanisms to achieve it.

Of course, separate deals (or deals with separate terms) can generate harm as well as benefits. A trade agreement between Vietnam and the United States, for example, will benefit Vietnam and its close ASEAN partners, but may divert trade from others. As integration proceeds, ASEAN should become better able to coordinate decisions, but, in the meantime, difficult tradeoffs will have to be made. Ultimately, centrality is in ASEAN's hands: the more open and integrated the region becomes, the more members will accept coordinated decision making (Petri and Vo 2012). In fact, initial policy differences in external policies may contribute to ASEAN integration by pressuring members to extend external preferences intraregionally, and by forcing internal partners to become more competitive.

How Centrality Affects External Partners

An integrated ASEAN is also likely to make a stronger economic partner and a more reliable political ally. It will offer more attractive markets and more efficient locations for production and investment. It is also likely to play a more constructive role as a counterweight to powers like China and the United States, which might otherwise dominate regional arrangements. Middle powers,

> *An integrated ASEAN is also likely to make a stronger economic partner and a more reliable political ally*

including ASEAN, South Korea, and Australia, often play constructive roles by emphasizing rules—in the terminology of political science, by socializing big powers (Johnston 2003). Rule-based solutions should help to make transactions more predictable and can help to defuse conflicts that arise in interactions with large powers.[8]

ASEAN centrality would clearly benefit external partners whose interests are complementary with the region's interests, such as the United States. Of course, interests are never fully aligned, and even complementary partners will be sometimes frustrated by their declining leverage over ASEAN policy. The benefits are more ambiguous for partners with more competitive economic and political interests, such as China. For them, the positive spillovers from ASEAN's success may be offset by the region's enhanced competitiveness and independence.

Centrality in Practice

While regional integration has clear objectives, it has consistently faced difficult practical hurdles. Current ASEAN initiatives reflect the experience of three decades of regional economic cooperation, and an even longer history of security cooperation. The EU faced similar challenges, but there are large differences between the EU and ASEAN projects. European states were more consistently developed and could focus on internal integration first. The Treaty of Rome (1957) and eventually the Single Market Programme (1986) prioritized consolidated internal positions and paved the way for a single authority, the European Commission, to manage internal and eventually also external economic issues. Europe also had to integrate economies with different comparative advantages, but ASEAN's diversity is, arguably, far greater.

The European Economic Community was a customs union from the outset, with the Common External Tariff adopted in 1957 superseding the tariff regimes of individual countries. Nevertheless, members participated independently in external negotiations, such as the Kennedy Round, until the Maastricht Treaty made the European Commission the exclusive authority for external negotiations in 1992. Since then, the EU has agreed to many FTAs, including one with South Korea in 2011, and is in the process of converting its "Lomé Agreements" with former colonies in Africa, the Caribbean, and the Pacific (ACP) into economic partnership agreements. It is also in talks with the United States to form a "Transatlantic Trade and Investment Partnership" (TTIP), which would be the biggest FTA in the world. The European Commission has become more effective in dealing with external partners and in promoting their joint interests in the General Agreement on Tariffs and Trade (GATT) and, eventually, the World Trade Organization (WTO).

In ASEAN, internal regional integration and extra-regional agreements are less clearly sequenced. This is partly due to early interests in bilateral and regional agreements, reflecting the importance of external ties compared to internal ones. These parallel internal and external integration efforts raise questions about interactions between them—can the two tracks reinforce each other, or will they make progress more difficult?

Internal Centrality: From the Bangkok Declaration to the AEC

Regional cooperation in ASEAN had to begin with politics. In the 1960s, the Cultural Revolution was underway in China; Indonesia and Malaysia were in conflict; and the war in Vietnam was heating up. Many members had recently gained independence and were deeply concerned about stability and regional peace. As the Bangkok Declaration put it, the parties were "mindful of the existence of mutual interests and common problems among countries of Southeast Asia and convinced of the need to strengthen further the existing bonds of regional solidarity and cooperation." The declaration aimed to establish a framework for such cooperation.

When ASEAN heads of state met at the first ASEAN Summit in 1976, a united front against communism was considered essential and led to the ASEAN Concord and the ASEAN Treaty of Amity and Cooperation. But over the next decade, the Southeast Asian political environment turned much more constructive with the gradual decline of regional conflicts, reform in China, and the dissolution of the Soviet Union. The region had an unprecedented opportunity to become more stable, and, in retrospect, it wisely exploited this window for cooperation.

Enlargement. ASEAN's first new mission was to bring all of Southeast Asia under its tent. The first expansion included the small, newly independent Brunei in 1984. The second, Vietnam, took longer. But in the mid-1980s, Vietnam took a sharp turn toward pragmatism—it adopted the *doi moi* program of market-oriented reforms in 1986, withdrew from Cambodia in 1989, and signed the ASEAN Treaty of Amity and Cooperation in 1991. The United States also facilitated this shift by lifting its trade embargo on Vietnam in 1994, and Vietnam entered ASEAN in 1995.

> *ASEAN has an exceptional record in helping regional economies enter the Asian mainstream*

In the mid-1990s, ASEAN leaders—led by the indefatigable Secretary General Ajit Singh— focused on adding Cambodia, Lao PDR, and Myanmar in ASEAN, despite the political and economic challenges involved. All joined by 1999. Only Timor-Leste and, perhaps, Papua New Guinea remain to be added. In short, ASEAN has an exceptional—and now near-complete— record in helping regional economies enter the Asian mainstream.

Economic integration. With enlargement approaching completion, economic cooperation is emerging as ASEAN's focus. An early ASEAN Preferential Trading Agreement (PTA) was signed in February 1977. The PTA was not ambitious—it took a positive-list approach to liberalization and offered only modest preferences, with one famous example involving preferences for regional trade in snowplows. Although the PTA switched to a negative list in 1984 and margins of preference were deepened in 1987, studies could not find significant trade effects. The same is true of the early stages of investment cooperation, including the ASEAN Industrial Projects, ASEAN Industrial Complementation, and ASEAN Industrial Joint Ventures programs. These initiatives were still based on the import substitution paradigm, and they promoted governmental industrialization schemes with little scope for private sector integration (Naya and Plummer 1991).

By the early 1990s, however, East Asian economic competition was in full force, and the Asia-Pacific Economic Cooperation (APEC) group, established in 1989, emerged as a potential competitor to ASEAN. Economics became the region's top priority, particularly in light of the end of the Cold War. This led initially to AFTA in 1992. Although it was initially restricted to ten manufacturing sectors with intraregional tariffs between 0–5 percent, AFTA was later expanded to include all goods (subject to exclusion lists) and no tariffs. AFTA is now fully implemented, except for in CLMV countries (Cambodia, Lao PDR, Myanmar, and Vietnam), which have additional time for adoption. Cooperation was further expanded with the ASEAN Investment Area in 1998 and the ASEAN Comprehensive Investment Agreement in 2012.

The ASEAN community. The framework for regional integration was gradually strengthened. In 2002, the ASEAN heads of government committed to creating an ASEAN community by 2020. This vision, comprising economic, political-security, and sociocultural pillars, was formalized in the Bali Accord II a year later. To strengthen its role in implementing this project, ASEAN adopted a new charter to become an international legal entity, which was ratified by member states in 2008.

These efforts ultimately aim to develop a borderless Southeast Asia, representing the first such large-scale integration project in the developing world. In this framework, the AEC would ensure the free flow of goods, services, and skilled labor, as well as freer capital movements. The deadline for implementing the AEC was moved up to 2015 in the Cebu Declaration of 2007, and the detailed ASEAN Economic Community Blueprint was drafted to guide its implementation (ASEAN 2007). The blueprint stipulated a timetable as well as a monitoring effort. An overview of its various components can be found in Table 3.

The AEC Blueprint defined four goals: (1) a Single Market and Production Base, based on the free flow of goods, services, investment, and skilled labor, and from freer flows of capital; (2) a Competitive Economic Region, based on commitments to competition policy, consumer protection, protection of intellectual property rights, infrastructure development, e-commerce, and avoidance of double taxation; (3) Equitable Economic Development, based on a strategy to close development gaps; and (4) Integration into the Global Economy, based on enhanced participation in the global trading system (Plummer and Chia 2009). The ASEAN Blueprint also calls for the development of a scorecard to measure implementation progress.

A borderless Southeast Asia would represent the first large-scale regional integration project in the developing world

Given these ambitious goals, it is not surprising that much still remains to be done.[9] Progress has been achieved on tariffs, however; since January 2010, 99 percent of ASEAN-6 (the original ASEAN economies and Brunei) total tariff lines had fallen to zero on intraregional trade.[10] For the transitional ASEAN countries, tariff levels were down to the 0–5 percent level by 2010, and they are on track to be eliminated by 2015. Thus, AFTA is essentially in place.

However, nontariff barriers to trade (NTBs) still constitute serious impediments to intraregional trade and FDI, even though they were supposed to be eliminated by 2012 for the ASEAN-6 (or 2018 for the transitional ASEAN economies). In addition, there continue to be problems associated with the implementation of the ASEAN Single Window, trade facilitation, technical barriers, trade logistics, and services liberalization, particularly for the transitional economies.

The record on trade in services is also mixed. There have been five rounds of services negotiations under the ASEAN Framework Agreement on Services (AFAS). These have made considerable progress on cross-border services liberalization (mode 1), but less in other areas. Deunden (2012) argues that even AEC's ambitions actually fall below what would be considered a unified market in services, especially

Table 3. Overview of the AEC Blueprint

Core Elements	Actions	Model Representation
A. Single Market and Production Base		
1. Goods	• Eliminate duties, NTBs, simplify rules of origin (ROOs) • Trade facilitation, customs integration, single window • Harmonize standards and regulations	• Lower tariffs • Lower goods nontariff barriers
2. Services	• Remove restrictions on service trade • Allow at least 70% equity participation • Schedule commitments for Mode 4 • Extend MRAs, liberalize financial services	• Lower service nontariff barriers • Higher FDI flows
3. Investment	• Investment protection, facilitation, liberalization • Nondiscrimination, national treatment	• Higher FDI flows
4. Capital	• Harmonize regulations • Promote cross-border capital raising	
5. Labor	• Facilitate movement of skilled and professional labor in cross-border trade • Enhance movement of students • Work toward harmonizing qualifications	• Lower service nontariff barriers
6. Priority sectors	• Projects in 12 priority sectors	
7. Food, agriculture, forestry	• Harmonize best practices, SPS, safety and quality standards, use of chemicals, and biotechnology • Promote technology transfer	• Lower goods nontariff barriers
B. Competitive Economic Region		
1. Competition policy	• Introduce competition policies and develop regional networks and guidelines	• Lower goods nontariff barriers
2. Consumer protection	• Develop regional networks and guidelines	

Table 3. Overview of the AEC Blueprint (continued)		
Core Elements	**Actions**	**Model Representation**
3. Intellectual property rights (IPR)	• Implement ASEAN IPR Action Plan • Promote regional cooperation	• Higher FDI flows
4. Infrastructure	• Facilitate multimodal transport, complete Singapore-Kunming rail link • Integrated maritime transport, open sky policies, single aviation market • High-speed IT interconnections • ASEAN power grid, gas pipelines	• Lower service nontariff barriers
5. Taxation	• Complete bilateral agreements	
6. E-commerce	• Best practices and harmonized legal infrastructure	• Lower service nontariff barriers
C. Equitable Economic Development		
1. Small and medium enterprises (SMEs)	• ASEAN Blueprint of best practices	
2. Initiative for integration	• Technical assistance and capacity building in CLMV countries	
D. Integration into the Global Economy		
1. Coherent approach	• Review FTA/CEP commitments • Establish coordination and common approaches	• FTAs with other economies
2. Supply networks	• International best practices and standards • Technical assistance	

Source: Based on ASEAN (2007).

with respect to commercial presence (mode 3) and the movement of natural persons (mode 4). With respect to FDI, ASEAN has committed to free and open investment by 2015, approving most favored nation and national treatment to all investors (with limited exceptions), fewer restrictions on priority sectors, and the removal of restrictive investment measures. However, achieving these goals continues to pose challenges in many ASEAN economies.

The ASEAN Summit in October 2013 determined that the region had completed 80 percent of the 259 measures included in the AEC Blueprint.[11] This is a difficult number to verify, and, in any event, the remaining 20 percent of measures will be especially challenging. The summit, therefore, recognized the need to develop a post-2015 program to continue progress on economic cooperation.[12]

External Centrality: From AFTA to Asia-Pacific Regionalism

Because even an integrated ASEAN would still be a small economy compared to many of its trade partners, the region needs to build stronger relationships with other economies in Asia and the West. These external integration efforts cannot wait until internal integration is complete, but are proceeding in parallel. Thus, ASEAN faces challenges that the European Community did not: it has to develop external relationships even though its ability to make common policy is limited.

As a result, the external trade policies of ASEAN members are not closely integrated. As an FTA rather than a customs union, ASEAN cannot set common tariffs. ASEAN's trade agreements with other partners (commonly referred to as ASEAN-Plus agreements) are mainly collections of bilateral negotiations, often conducted in parallel, with little exchange of information. In fact, many members have independently forged accords with nonmembers.

> *External integration efforts cannot wait until internal integration is complete, but will need to proceed in parallel*

The prescription of centrality is an effort to contain this process in order to develop greater external leverage.

ASEAN's external integration efforts have proceeded in two major phases. The first focused on external relationships based on ASEAN-Plus

FTAs with partners mainly in Asia, but extending beyond Asia as well. The second phase, now underway, involves two major regional cooperation initiatives, one spanning the Asia-Pacific region, and another among Asian economies.

ASEAN-Plus agreements. Individual ASEAN member countries have concluded 28 FTAs with non-ASEAN countries.[13] Some, such as the Singapore-US FTA, are deeper than the ASEAN trade regime. There are now five ASEAN-Plus agreements; with China (2005); South Korea (2007); Japan (2008); India (2010); and Australia and New Zealand (2010). (Note that these countries are also the non-ASEAN members of the RCEP by design.) Others are being negotiated, including with the EU.

An important feature of these agreements is that they are negotiated by member states in parallel with the external dialogue partner. The ASEAN Secretariat does not have the capacity to lead, or even closely monitor, negotiations at this time, and members are often concerned that they do not have adequate information about the offers being considered by other members (Petri 2009). Thus, it is not surprising that ASEAN's bilateral agreements, and even its "ASEAN-Plus-One" agreements for various ASEAN members, vary in scope and coverage.

Trans-Pacific cooperation. Broader initiatives in the Asia-Pacific region have focused on two approaches: a trans-Pacific approach that includes the United States and other Eastern Pacific countries, and an Asia-only approach within ASEAN's network of dialogue partners. Divisions between these approaches first emerged in the 1990s when, on the one hand, the APEC forum was created and, on the other, Malaysian Prime Minister Mahathir Mohammed proposed an alternative East Asian Economic Group (EAEG) mechanism. Over time, these paths have crystallized into the current TPP and RCEP negotiations, respectively.

APEC was launched in a 1989 conference convened by Prime Minister Robert Hawke of Australia. The plan for APEC initially excluded Canada and the United States, but US Secretary of State James Baker worried that the conference would "draw a line down the middle of the Pacific" and lobbied for including the United States. Meanwhile, concerned that the new grouping would be dominated by developed countries, ASEAN ultimately gained a role for its secretary general in the APEC coordinating committee. The EAEG was amended to become the East Asian Economic Caucus, and ultimately disappeared.

APEC now includes 21 economies: the United States, Canada, Mexico, Chile, and Peru in the Americas; Japan, South Korea, Russia, China, Taiwan, Hong Kong, and seven ASEAN economies in East Asia; and Papua New Guinea, New Zealand, and Australia in Oceania.[14] In 1994, APEC adopted the Bogor Goals, pledging to create a region of "open trade and investment" by 2010 (2020 for developing member economies). Although APEC has received much credit for progress in trade facilitation and for developing a rich consultative network among member governments, its more ambitious goals have yet to be achieved.

To promote faster progress, four small APEC economies—Brunei, Chile, Singapore, and New Zealand—developed a high-quality FTA (the Trans-Pacific Strategic Economic Partnership agreement, also known as the P4), to which they hoped to attract other APEC countries. Several countries agreed to join in 2008, including the United States, and the initiative has now expanded to the current 12-country TPP negotiations. Four ASEAN members—Brunei, Malaysia, Singapore, and Vietnam—are among those negotiating, while several others, especially the Philippines and Thailand, have expressed interest.

Asia-centered cooperation. Meanwhile, ASEAN's regional diplomacy has created a formidable network of agreements in Asia and Oceania. In an effort to leverage this network into genuine regional leadership in trade, ASEAN is now committed to developing it into a true pan-Asian integration framework through the RCEP. This effort

Regional integration frameworks can help to consolidate the 'noodle bowl' of existing arrangements

will also help to consolidate the "noodle bowl" of existing arrangements in order to exploit the advantages of larger economic zones.

Pan-Asian integration initially emerged in the form of two approaches: an ASEAN-Plus-Three grouping (including China, Japan, and South Korea) and an ASEAN-Plus-Six grouping (including also

Australia, New Zealand, and India). The ASEAN-Plus-Three was launched in 2004, when economic ministers commissioned a feasibility study of a potential East Asia FTA. ASEAN then established an East Asia Summit (EAS) in 2005, adding Australia, New Zealand, and India to the ASEAN-Plus-Three meetings, to address concerns that the dialogue was too heavily dominated by China. In 2007, Japan proposed negotiations to create an FTA based on the EAS, named the Comprehensive Economic Partnership of East Asia. Although the EAS agreed to examine both frameworks in parallel in 2009, disagreements between China and Japan prevented significant progress.

At the 2011 ASEAN Summit, China and Japan agreed to move forward on both tracks and jointly proposed working groups to shape the negotiations. ASEAN, in turn, decided to develop a template of its own, later formalized as the RCEP at the ASEAN Summit in November 2012. With negotiations now underway, the initiative has become a powerful symbol of ASEAN centrality. But its success will depend on many unknowns, including whether a critical missing piece—a meaningful agreement among China, Japan, and South Korea—can be concluded within the RCEP framework.

The Benefits of Internal and External Integration

While policymakers could reasonably expect that ASEAN integration would produce significant gains, relatively little work has been done on the likely quantitative effects. In a recent study (Petri et al. 2012a), a comprehensive general equilibrium model was applied to estimate the implications of the ASEAN project, addressing both the internal and external integration initiatives that are under consideration. The results confirm substantial gains, reaching up to 12 percent to the region's GDP, or 1–2 percentage points to its GDP growth rate over the implementation period.

The model was used to estimate the effects of several distinct phases of the internal integration project, as well as additional steps for leveraging the region's internal efforts through new (or better) agreements with countries outside the region. The results show large gains from each of these steps.

The analysis involved the following policy simulations:

1. AFTA: completion of AFTA by reducing all remaining tariffs on intra-ASEAN trade
2. AFTA+: intensification of AFTA by removing NTBs, including regulatory barriers such as diverging standards and testing requirements (lacking detailed information on these measures, the simulation assumes a horizontal reduction of trade costs equal to 5 percent of trade values)
3. AEC: further reforms that improve the investment climate, modeled via increasing FDI inflows to levels similar to those in the most open ASEAN countries (see Petri et al. 2012a for details)
4. AEC+: additional bilateral FTAs with other RCEP economies
5. AEC++: additional bilateral FTAs with the United States and the EU

The structure of the model is presented in Box 1; how various features of the AEC are included in the model is summarized in the final column of Table 3; and the results of various scenarios are presented in Table 4. The variable reported in this table is a summary measure of national income gains under alternative scenarios, based on assumptions about integration policies. The full implementation of the AEC would raise real incomes by $69.4 billion, or 5.3 percent of regional GDP over the 2004 baseline—a large number compared to those usually estimated in FTA studies. This study attributes much of the increase to features of the AEC that go beyond AFTA; the effects of the full AEC are seven times as large as those attributable to remaining liberalization under AFTA.

Roughly half of the additional benefits come from trade facilitation (the difference between AFTA and AFTA+), and half from investment facilitation (the presumed difference between AFTA+ and the AEC).

All ASEAN members would gain from the AEC

All ASEAN members would gain from the AEC, with the largest countries experiencing the greatest absolute gains. The benefits are not related to per capita income levels; for example, Cambodia and Singapore, countries at opposite ends of the ASEAN income spectrum, both have large gains.

The benefits of the AEC are, therefore, considerable, but since ASEAN does three-quarters of its trade with, and receives four-fifths of its FDI from, nonmember countries, scenarios that also include other Asian partners, the United States, and the EU generate still greater gains. FTAs with major partners more than double the benefits of the AEC to $151 billion, or 11.6 percent of GDP. Slightly more than half of the additional benefits would come from agreements with RCEP partners, and slightly less than half from agreements with the United States and Europe. The benefits from deepening external integration are larger, as expected, for ASEAN economies with the strongest linkages outside the region (for example, Malaysia, Thailand, and Vietnam) and smaller for those that are mainly regionally oriented (for example, Brunei and Lao PDR).

The importance of extra-regional integration effects helps to explain why inward-looking economic integration—a plausible goal in Europe due to the intensity of its regional trade—was never a viable option for ASEAN. Although early ASEAN cooperation also emerged when import substitution theories were in vogue, it only produced token initiatives for protected, inward-looking development. This was fortuitous; an inward-looking AFTA could well have met the same fate as the Latin American Free Trade Area, which went into effect in the early 1960s and collapsed in the 1970s. Instead, the AEC's provisions that support integration into the global economy remain some of the most successful dimensions of the AEC project.

The TPP and the RCEP

Although the AEC and other key intra-ASEAN projects are not yet completed, ASEAN now also finds itself at the intersection of two of the world's most important megaregional trade initiatives, the TPP and the RCEP. This section examines ASEAN's challenges in responding to these large opportunities, while also trying to reconcile them with its own integration process. These objectives have implications not only for the region itself, but also for the policies of its key external partners.

Economics of FTAs

The economic logic of an FTA highlights some of the difficulties facing ASEAN, which confronts complex internal and external liberalization choices. While nondiscriminatory liberalization is widely

Box 1: The Computable General Equilibrium Model

Computable general equilibrium (CGE) analysis takes account of interactions among a wide range of markets and provides quantitative answers to policy questions about integration. The crux of the analysis is to calculate prices, production, and demand levels that make expenditures equal incomes, and supply equal demand in many markets and countries. To calculate the equilibrium, prices are assumed to adjust until consumers have chosen a desired basket of goods given their incomes, firms have set production at levels that maximize profits, and the demand for factors of production equals available endowments. CGE models simulate FTAs by introducing the effects of policy changes (such as tariff reductions) into a pre-agreement equilibrium and adjusting prices until a new equilibrium is reached.

CGE analysis uses data from a benchmark year, and its mathematical modeling is based on neoclassical assumptions about the motivation of economic agents, market structure, consumer preferences, and production technology. These assumptions are coded as mathematical relationships and contain parameters that capture behavioral relationships, including elasticities (which measure the responsiveness of one variable to changes in another) and production and demand parameters—for example, the share of food consumption in total consumption demand. The parameters of the mathematical model are calibrated to make the baseline solution match real-world data in a benchmark year.

The predictions of economic theory about trade policy often depend on such empirical parameters. CGE models enable policymakers to assess such quantitative impacts. For example, in the case of FTAs, "trade creation" (generated by a more efficient division of labor within the trade area) and "trade diversion" (generated by inefficiencies that result from discrimination against outsiders) have opposing effects, and the net effect may be positive or negative. CGE models can quantify the magnitudes of these effects and estimate net welfare results.

Our CGE model is based on a new type of global trade model developed by Fan Zhai (2008). A new feature of the model is that it incorporates recent innovations in heterogeneous firms trade theory into the CGE framework. The firms of most sectors in the model are heterogeneous in productivity, enabling the model to reflect intra-industry changes that occur when, for example, trade liberalization enables the most productive firms to export more and expand, and the least productive to contract in the face of stiffer import competition. Given the fixed cost of exporting, the model is also able to capture both the intensive margins (more trade of already traded products) and extensive margins (trade in products not traded previously).

This model is especially appropriate for assessing the implications of deep integration efforts. Its demand structure enables it to track the effects of additional varieties of goods on consumer welfare; its scale-sensitive production function allows it to track productivity gains associated with the growth of firms; and its treatment of productivity variations makes it possible to track the shift in production from relatively unproductive firms to relatively productive ones. The specification of the model is described in Petri et al. (2012b).

Table 4. Effects of ASEAN Integration Scenarios Relative to Baseline, 2015

	Income gains ($bill)					Percentage change from baseline				
	AFTA	AFTA+	AEC	AEC+	AEC++	AFTA	AFTA+	AEC	AEC+	AEC++
ASEAN	**10.1**	**38.0**	**69.4**	**115.6**	**151.0**	**0.78**	**2.92**	**5.34**	**8.89**	**11.61**
Brunei	0.2	0.4	0.5	0.6	0.7	2.56	5.38	7.00	9.29	10.62
Cambodia	0.3	0.5	0.6	0.7	1.2	2.74	5.42	6.26	7.23	12.34
Indonesia	1.0	6.2	27.6	36.5	43.2	0.22	1.40	6.21	8.21	9.71
Lao PDR	0.0	0.1	0.2	0.2	0.2	0.63	2.50	3.59	3.76	4.56
Myanmar	0.0	0.2	0.6	0.7	1.4	0.33	1.22	4.39	4.80	9.31
Malaysia	2.7	2.9	5.7	21.1	27.9	1.41	1.55	2.99	11.16	14.70
Philippines	0.9	2.2	4.5	4.4	5.9	0.61	1.59	3.24	3.16	4.29
Singapore	2.6	14.0	15.1	18.1	19.0	1.64	9.00	9.68	11.59	12.16
Thailand	1.6	9.8	12.2	19.5	25.8	0.65	3.93	4.90	7.82	10.38
Vietnam	0.9	1.6	2.4	13.8	25.7	1.10	1.81	2.82	16.00	29.83
Partners	**0.9**	**-17.4**	**-16.9**	**28.4**	**17.9**	**0.00**	**-0.04**	**-0.04**	**0.07**	**0.04**
China	0.4	-4.6	-7.8	-6.5	-12.2	0.01	-0.10	-0.16	-0.14	-0.26
Japan	0.1	-1.3	-1.6	9.2	7.3	0.00	-0.02	-0.03	0.17	0.14
Korea	-0.2	-1.4	-2.7	10.6	9.1	-0.02	-0.15	-0.27	1.07	0.92

Table 4. Effects of ASEAN Integration Scenarios Relative to Baseline, 2015 (continued)

	Income gains ($bill)					Percentage change from baseline					
	AFTA	AFTA+	AEC	AEC+	AEC++	AFTA	AFTA+	AEC	AEC+	AEC++
India	0.8	0.1	-0.8	23.9	23.5	0.06	0.01	-0.06	1.67	1.64
Australia	0.0	-0.2	0.2	0.3	0.1	0.00	-0.02	0.03	0.03	0.01
New Zealand	-0.1	-0.1	-0.1	-0.1	-0.2	-0.05	-0.07	-0.08	-0.05	-0.15
United States	0.2	-2.8	-1.8	-3.7	-3.6	0.00	-0.02	-0.01	-0.03	-0.03
Europe	-0.3	-7.1	-2.3	-5.4	-6.2	0.00	-0.05	-0.01	-0.04	-0.04
Other Economies	**0.3**	**-1.1**	**0.2**	**-0.5**	**-2.1**	**0.00**	**-0.01**	**0.00**	**0.00**	**-0.02**
World	**11.4**	**19.4**	**52.7**	**143.4**	**166.8**	**0.02**	**0.04**	**0.10**	**0.26**	**0.30**

Source: Petri, Plummer, and Zhai 2012a.

understood to have robust positive effects, it is less obvious that partial liberalization, whether in the context of the AEC or through FTAs such as the TPP and RCEP, will benefit even the countries involved, much less their neighbors. From a theoretical viewpoint, regional agreements are second-best policy options, and could have either positive or negative effects depending on their empirical characteristics. This paper argues, however, that these agreements have special features that are likely to lead to positive-sum results and, hence, are attractive for ASEAN.

Not all experts see it this way. Some have argued that the mega-regional arrangements now emerging in the Asia-Pacific region are major threats to the world trading system and the WTO because they (1) violate principles of nondiscrimination and result in inefficient production, (2) contribute to the costly "noodle bowl" of bilateral FTAs, and (3) divert attention and resources from concluding the global Doha Development Agenda.

These arguments are valid up to a point—multilateral negotiations would be preferable to regional ones. But the driver of current regional negotiations is the failure of the global decision-making system, not the rise of divisive regionalism. The WTO's membership—159 diverse countries—and its comprehensive and consensual structure have made it impossible, for nearly two decades, to make any significant progress on new rules, despite dramatic changes in the structure and patterns of world trade and investment. These problems were in clear view at the WTO Ninth Ministerial Meeting in Bali, Indonesia, in December 2013, when essentially one country—India—threatened to prevent any accord from materializing due to its insistence on being able to use agricultural subsidies without any restrictions if used for "food security" purposes. A compromise was ultimately reached that satisfied India in the final scheduled day of the meetings, only to be met by a new complaint by Cuba—supported by Nicaragua, Venezuela, and Bolivia—that would force the United States to remove its trade embargo, a political non-starter. In the end, an accord was finally reached in overtime, the first

> *The driver of current regional negotiations is the failure of the global decision-making system, not the rise of divisive regionalism*

significant fruits of the Doha Development Agenda in the form of a mini-package covering aspects of trade facilitation, agriculture, and development-related issues. It was an historic agreement--without the mini-package, Doha may have been declared dead—but it was also a reminder that any "deep" liberalization in the context of such a diverse group of countries is increasingly difficult, exacerbated by the consensual nature of the WTO.

In effect, these difficulties at the multilateral level have led to a proliferation of small, bilateral trade agreements. Even if megaregionalism is second best to global rule making, it is likely to be better than the "noodle bowl" of roughly 300 bilateral FTAs that have consequently emerged.

Unlike the bilateral agreements of recent years, today's megaregionals are vast and reasonably inclusive, and they often overlap in membership and are aggressively seeking additional partners. The TPP, for example, has already grown to three times its original membership, and most of its members also participate in other megaregional negotiations. The TPP will generate more liberalization and less discrimination than most of the bilateral agreements it will replace. The larger FTAs now in negotiation are likely to produce much better results than previous bilateral agreements, and are also likely to reduce trade diversion and increase utilization rates (Kawai and Wignaraja 2011).

While the traditional theory on FTAs (Lipsey 1960, Viner 1950) focuses on the threat of trade and investment diversion, current megaregionals, according to the best available estimates, are significantly positive-sum initiatives. Moreover, an important contribution by Murray C. Kemp and Henry Y. Wan (1976) suggests that *all* negative outcomes can be avoided in such a setting. They show that for every customs union "there exists a common tariff vector and a system of lump-sum compensatory payments, involving only members of the union, such that there is an associated tariff-ridden competitive equilibrium in which each individual, whether a member of the union or not, is not worse off than before the formation of the union." In nontechnical terms, the members of a customs union can guarantee that outsiders will not be harmed by their discriminatory agreement by adjusting third-party tariffs (reducing protection on the imports of third countries) and, perhaps, by making internal transfers.

The Kemp-Wan result—an elegant, short theorem—was developed under restrictive conditions and applies, as originally proved, to customs unions rather than free trade areas. Nevertheless, its results are intuitive and can be carried over to many more complicated settings. The core argument is that the members of a trade agreement can adjust their relations with third countries to compensate for any negative effects of the agreement. Typically, this means lowering barriers facing third parties. If these adjustments then reshuffle the benefits within the agreement, member countries can find ways to compensate each other to make sure that no member is worse off. In the case of the EU, such a mechanism is provided by the EU structural funds. For the AEC, the "equitable economic region" pillar of the AEC Blueprint reflects this objective (although it does not provide a funding mechanism).

The Kemp-Wan theorem has direct applications to agreements that might be concluded by subsets of ASEAN economies with external partners. Such agreements are likely to be valuable to their members (for example, because they are more developed or more specialized in the production of advanced manufactures or services). The theorem, in turn, suggests ways of complementing such agreements with policies that avoid harm to other ASEAN members. Compensation could be financed and implemented by either the benefiting ASEAN economies and/or their external partners. The combination of liberalization and compensation, appropriately designed, would ultimately benefit all ASEAN members.

> *The Kemp-Wan theorem suggests ways of complementing agreements with policies that avoid harm to other ASEAN members*

The possibility that discriminatory liberalization can generate benefits without causing harm is also recognized by the GATT. Article 24 permits FTAs provided that they remove barriers to regional trade on substantially all goods within a reasonable period of time, and that participants refrain from increasing protection against third parties. These rules do not necessarily achieve the Kemp-Wan objectives (indeed, they were written before the theorem was published), but they strictly limit FTAs to those seriously intended to create trade in order to minimize the number of agreements that might harm other countries.

Implications of the TPP and the RCEP

In this section, further evidence will be presented that the current megaregional agreements are likely to generate significant benefits. These would come on top of the benefits of deeper integration within the ASEAN zone, and would also exceed the benefits of ASEAN-Plus-One agreements, as outlined in the previous section. The agreements would engage the region (especially those countries that participate in external agreements) in wider and potentially more dynamic international trading zones. As an example, the TPP aims to:

- Eliminate most tariffs and quantitative restrictions within a fixed time frame in all member economies. However, negotiators may adopt flexible implementation periods in order to avoid outright exceptions.
- Address trade issues that have emerged since the Uruguay Round. These include new policy challenges created by electronic commerce, the fragmentation of production in modern supply chains, and the rise of state-owned enterprises.
- Attract support from both developed and developing countries—a mix that the Doha Development Agenda is finding difficult to reach—without introducing special and differential treatment. Thus, the agreement is likely to have something for many sectors (primary goods, manufacturing, and services) and many interests (intellectual property, investment, and labor).
- Reach behind the border to make regulations more transparent and easier to navigate, including by smaller enterprises. This will require provisions on transparency and regulatory oversight, and on ways to set reasonable product standards, along with labor and environmental rules. The relevance of some of these issues is questioned by economists, but they cannot be ignored in democracies. Technology transfers and capacity building play similar roles for emerging economies.

As with any agreement, the TPP accord will be ultimately a compromise between provisions that genuinely advance integration and those that secure political support. Trade agreements are hammered out by policymakers. Hence, trade policy ultimately reflects political considerations, but even these can usually be designed to enhance trade and investment, or at least to be economically neutral. In any case, the potential advantages from integration are large enough to justify compromises, and estimates made in this paper suggest widespread benefits even if some economic goals are not achieved.

The RCEP has a different history than the TPP. It is a regional effort rather than a negotiation among like-minded countries, and it follows nearly a decade of attempts to initiate similar negotiations. In addition, the RCEP will overlap ASEAN-Plus-One agreements between ASEAN and all RCEP partners, and these have presumably already tested the limits of regional liberalization. Thus, the RCEP has important hurdles to overcome in order to improve on the status quo.

Still, the guidelines for the RCEP adopted by ASEAN (2012) are ambitious and envision a modern, comprehensive agreement, covering many of the areas addressed by the TPP. However, the guidelines also note that "the RCEP will include appropriate forms of flexibility including provision for special and differential treatment" (ASEAN 2012). Many observers applaud this commitment, but it will make it difficult to move beyond existing agreements. So far, negotiators have resisted including special and differential treatment in the TPP.

The most important missing piece in the RCEP is an agreement among China, Japan, and South Korea (CJK).[15] These countries have recently concluded a trilateral investment treaty and have started negotiations on a trilateral FTA. China and South Korea also have advanced bilateral trade negotiations underway. The CJK FTA would make the RCEP a far more important agreement than it is without such a deal. To be sure, it might also threaten ASEAN centrality. Not only would it erode preferences to ASEAN that are now incorporated in ASEAN-Plus-One agreements, but it would also give Northeast Asia a large stake in negotiating the terms of the RCEP and in managing its implementation. But all of these outcomes

> *The most important missing piece in the RCEP is an agreement among China, Japan, and South Korea*

depend on the progress of the CJK negotiations, which faces familiar political challenges.

Estimates of the implications of the TPP and RCEP agreements were made by modeling their potential economic effects relative to baseline projections, which include, for example, the implementation of the AEC. This is difficult—in addition to the usual uncertainties in economic modeling, the exact policy shocks are not yet known. A CGE model (as described in Box 1) was used in an effort to go beyond the usual simulation exercises, and to also include firm heterogeneity and FDI effects.

The baseline solution reflects projections of the Asia-Pacific economy developed by the Centre d'Etudes Prospectives et d'Informations Internationales (CEPII) (Foure, Benassy-Quere, and Fontagne 2010). It includes expected growth rates that will change the structure of the future world economy, the many FTAs that have been agreed upon but are not yet fully implemented, and policies that will deepen ASEAN integration.

Future agreements are modeled by assuming that their liberalization effects can be described by the parameters of existing FTAs. For example, past North American and ASEAN FTAs are used, respectively, to "predict" the TPP and the RCEP agreements. Two variants of the TPP agreement are examined: the current 12-country configuration and an alternative with 16 countries, which includes Indonesia, the Philippines, and Thailand—the major ASEAN economies that are missing from the TPP12. Finally, an extended, regionwide agreement is also examined, based on the membership of APEC which has proposed a Free Trade Area of the Asia Pacific (FTAAP) to begin negotiations in 2020, plus India, also a RCEP member. The provisions of this agreement, denoted FTAAPX in this study, are represented with a hybrid template that splits the difference between the templates of the TPP and the RCEP. The results are discussed below and are also published in more detail at www.asiapacifictrade.org.

All scenarios produce substantial benefits, with global income gains ranging from $233 billion annually for the TPP12 to $2.3 trillion for the regionwide FTAAPX. This latter scenario would increase world GDP by 2 percent, much more than has been estimated for the effects of completing the Doha Development Agenda. To be sure, a large part of these benefits would be captured by the largest economies participating in these agreements—China, India, Japan, and the United States.

Results for ASEAN are shown at the bottom of Tables 5 and 6.[16] The current TPP12 would generate modest gains for ASEAN as a whole, but large gains for the four ASEAN economies included in it. However, the TPP16 agreement, which would include all but the least developed ASEAN members, would generate large benefits for ASEAN ($218 billion or 6 percent of GDP), nearly three times those from the RCEP ($78 billion and 2 percent of GDP). Differences between the TPP12 and the TPP16 suggest that Indonesia, the Philippines, and Thailand—countries that have been reluctant to commit to the TPP so far—will be under considerable economic pressure to join if the agreement goes forward.

The ranking of the two agreements is similar for all ASEAN members, with the advantages of the TPP16 over the RCEP ranging from roughly two-to-one (for Malaysia) to more than five-to-one (for Singapore). The TPP is estimated to have a large advantage over the RCEP because it (1) applies deeper integration measures that lead to greater efficiency gains, and (2) offers preferential access to new markets, such as the North American Free Trade Agreement (NAFTA). Currently, ASEAN has FTAs in place with all RCEP economies, even before the conclusion of the RCEP.

For ASEAN members, the regionwide FTAAPX agreement would generate only small additional gains beyond the TPP. In fact, some ASEAN members, including Indonesia, the Philippines, and Thailand, would gain more from the TPP than from the FTAAPX. This is because the FTAAPX would include China and India, and thus enable those countries to compete in the Americas on the same terms as ASEAN countries, eroding ASEAN's preferences under the TPP.

Overall, the simulations yield the somewhat unexpected but quantitatively significant result that, for ASEAN members, the RCEP would have to be very ambitious to compete with the TPP.[17] It would have to have much more rigorous provisions than typical ASEAN trade agreements, as well as innovations that generate greater utilization of agreements. A "business as usual" FTA would add little to the agreements that already exist.

Overall, the TPP is an attractive option for countries willing to accept its challenging terms, and should have indirect effects that also benefit ASEAN integration. The regional debate often avoids these issues, emphasizing instead the advantages of flexibility in reaching agreements. But the ease of *negotiating* an agreement is usually negatively correlated with the *benefits* that flow from it. Flexibility may help negotiators make progress, but often at the cost of avoiding the hard decisions that lead to productive trade

> *The ease of* negotiating *an agreement is usually negatively correlated with the benefits that flow from it*

and investment results. This trade-off is well recognized in China, where the *Global Times* recently noted that deep integration is needed to advance reform (Liu 2013). The article concluded that the "TPP brings challenges, but the challenges do not lie in 'being surrounded,' but in the impetus for China to take solid actions."

Why Not Both?

The TPP and the RCEP are often discussed as alternatives, but that is not the case. Several ASEAN economies already participate in both negotiations—Brunei, Malaysia, Singapore, and Vietnam—and there is no reason why other middle-income countries should not do so as well. (The immediate prospects for participating in the TPP are less promising for the region's least developed countries, but in time their involvement is also possible.) Even if other ASEAN countries cannot join the current phase of negotiations, the agreement is likely to anticipate enlargement and provide a path for accession. For countries willing to commit to both agreements—and hopefully the terms will be within reach for most—the strategy of dual membership is attractive.

Tables 5 and 6 do not show the exact benefits of participating in both tracks, which will be slightly less than the sum of the TPP and RCEP simulations, due to overlapping provisions and other economic effects. For the most part, however, the TPP and the RCEP offer benefits that are largely complementary—one focuses on deeper integration with the Americas, and the other on improved access to Asian markets. The authors' experiments show that benefits from participating in both agreements are roughly 90 percent of the sum of benefits from participating in one at a time—that is, from the sum of the TPP and RCEP columns of Table 5.

Table 5. Income Effects of TPP, RCEP, and FTAAP

Economy	GDP 2025 (bill. 2007 dollars)	Income gains (bill. 2007 dollars)				Percent change from baseline			
		TPP12	TPP16	RCEP	FTAAPX	TPP12	TPP16	RCEP	FTAAPX
Americas	**24,867**	**101.7**	**160.8**	**2.5**	**412.4**	**0.41**	**0.65**	**0.01**	**1.66**
Canada	1,978	8.7	12.4	-0.1	29.7	0.44	0.63	0.00	1.50
Chile	292	2.5	3.5	0.0	7.6	0.86	1.20	0.00	2.61
Mexico	2,004	9.9	31.2	2.8	73.7	0.50	1.56	0.14	3.68
Peru	320	3.9	5.4	0.0	6.2	1.22	1.69	-0.02	1.93
United States	20,273	76.6	108.2	-0.1	295.2	0.38	0.53	0.00	1.46
Asia	**34,901**	**125.2**	**299.8**	**627.0**	**1658.6**	**0.36**	**0.86**	**1.80**	**4.75**
Brunei	20	0.2	0.4	1.2	1.6	0.95	1.84	5.85	7.64
China	17,249	-34.8	-82.4	249.7	699.9	-0.20	-0.48	1.45	4.06
Hong Kong	406	-0.5	-1.3	46.8	88.4	-0.12	-0.32	11.54	21.77
India	5,233	-2.7	-6.9	91.3	226.2	-0.05	-0.13	1.74	4.32
Indonesia	1,549	-2.2	62.2	17.7	41.3	-0.14	4.02	1.14	2.67
Japan	5,338	104.6	128.8	95.8	227.9	1.96	2.41	1.79	4.27
South Korea	2,117	-2.8	50.2	82.0	131.8	-0.13	2.37	3.87	6.23
Malaysia	431	24.2	30.1	14.2	43.5	5.61	6.98	3.29	10.09
Philippines	322	-0.8	22.1	7.6	17.4	-0.24	6.88	2.35	5.42

Table 5. Income Effects of TPP, RCEP, and FTAAP (continued)

Economy	GDP 2025 (bill. 2007 dollars)	Income gains (bill. 2007 dollars)				Percent change from baseline			
		TPP12	TPP16	RCEP	FTAAPX	TPP12	TPP16	RCEP	FTAAPX
Singapore	415	7.9	12.3	2.4	18.1	1.90	2.97	0.58	4.37
Taiwan	840	-1.0	-6.4	-16.1	53.7	-0.12	-0.76	-1.92	6.39
Thailand	558	-2.4	42.5	15.5	30.0	-0.44	7.61	2.79	5.38
Vietnam	340	35.7	48.7	17.3	75.3	10.52	14.34	5.10	22.15
Other ASEAN	83	-0.4	-0.5	1.6	3.5	-0.42	-0.58	1.88	4.19
Oceania	1,634	10.7	14.6	21.7	36.5	0.65	0.89	1.33	2.23
Australia	1,433	6.6	9.8	19.8	30.1	0.46	0.68	1.38	2.10
New Zealand	201	4.1	4.7	1.9	6.4	2.02	2.36	0.92	3.16
Others	41,820	-14.1	-24.2	-6.8	172.2	-0.03	-0.06	-0.02	0.41
Europe	22,714	-3.7	-4.9	5.1	-36.4	-0.02	-0.02	0.02	-0.16
Russia	2,865	-1.4	-3.0	-5.3	287.5	-0.05	-0.10	-0.18	10.04
Rest of World	16,241	-9.0	-16.3	-6.6	-79.0	-0.06	-0.10	-0.04	-0.49
WORLD	103,223	223.4	450.9	644.4	2279.6	0.22	0.44	0.62	2.21
Memorandum									
ASEAN	3,718	62.2	217.8	77.5	230.7	1.67	5.86	2.08	6.20

Source: Authors' simulations.
Note: FTAAPX includes all economies that are members of TPP, RCEP, and/or APEC.

Table 6. Export Effects of TPP, RCEP, and FTAAP

Economy	Exports 2025 (bill. 2007 dollars)	Export gains (bill. 2007 dollars)				Percent change from baseline			
		TPP12	TPP16	RCEP	FTAAPX	TPP12	TPP16	RCEP	FTAAPX
Americas	**4,163**	**166.1**	**260.2**	**-8.1**	**781.9**	**4.0**	**6.3**	**-0.2**	**18.8**
Canada	597	13.8	17.7	-2.4	34.0	2.3	3.0	-0.4	5.7
Chile	151	3.7	4.5	-1.3	9.2	2.4	3.0	-0.8	6.1
Mexico	507	19.1	40.1	-0.5	102.3	3.8	7.9	-0.1	20.2
Peru	95	6.0	7.4	-0.2	10.6	6.3	7.8	-0.3	11.1
United States	2,813	123.5	190.5	-3.7	625.9	4.4	6.8	-0.1	22.3
Asia	**10,403**	**186.6**	**517.8**	**1420.0**	**3434.5**	**1.8**	**5.0**	**13.7**	**33.0**
Brunei	9	0.2	0.3	0.9	1.2	2.6	3.8	10.5	13.3
China	4,597	-43.7	-107.8	638.3	1590.1	-1.0	-2.3	13.9	34.6
Hong Kong	235	-1.3	-3.6	39.9	73.9	-0.6	-1.5	17.0	31.5
India	869	-5.2	-13.2	237.9	536.1	-0.6	-1.5	27.4	61.7
Indonesia	501	-3.9	98.3	52.6	119.3	-0.8	19.6	10.5	23.8
Japan	1,252	139.7	202.5	225.1	419.0	11.2	16.2	18.0	33.5
South Korea	718	-7.0	94.5	173.6	244.2	-1.0	13.2	24.2	34.0
Malaysia	336	40.0	44.2	20.2	56.1	11.9	13.2	6.0	16.7
Philippines	163	-1.4	33.5	10.8	27.5	-0.9	20.6	6.6	16.8

Table 6. Export Effects of TPP, RCEP, and FTAAP (continued)

Economy	Exports 2025 (bill. 2007 dollars)	Export gains (bill. 2007 dollars)				Percent change from baseline				
		TPP12	TPP16	RCEP	FTAAPX	TPP12	TPP16	RCEP	FTAAPX	
Singapore	712	-4.0	-17.5	-40.3	-5.0	-0.6	-2.5	-5.7	-1.9	
Taiwan	476	-5.1	82.7	34.7	150.8	-1.1	17.4	7.3	21.2	
Thailand	263	11.3	13.3	-5.7	74.6	4.3	5.1	-2.2	15.7	
Vietnam	239	67.9	92.1	29.9	139.3	28.4	38.6	12.5	58.3	
Other ASEAN	34	-0.9	-1.6	2.1	7.3	-2.7	-4.6	6.2	21.6	
Oceania	**392**	**15.2**	**20.4**	**45.5**	**65.5**	**3.9**	**5.2**	**11.6**	**16.7**	
Australia	332	11.1	15.7	42.8	59.0	3.4	4.7	12.9	17.8	
New Zealand	60	4.1	4.7	2.7	6.5	6.8	7.8	4.4	10.8	
Others	13,457	-62.7	-143.7	-73.7	-233.9	-0.5	-1.1	-0.5	-1.7	
Europe	7,431	-32.2	-75.6	-41.6	-328.9	-0.4	-1.0	-0.6	-4.4	
Russia	1,071	-3.6	-9.3	-6.2	334.8	-0.3	-0.9	-0.6	31.3	
Rest of World	**4,955**	**-26.9**	**-58.8**	**-25.9**	**-239.7**	**-0.5**	**-1.2**	**-0.5**	**-4.8**	
WORLD	**28,415**	**305.2**	**654.7**	**1383.7**	**4048.0**	**1.1**	**2.3**	**4.9**	**14.2**	
Memorandum										
ASEAN	2,021	108.2	362.9	145.5	420.3	5.4	18.0	7.2	20.8	

Source: Authors' simulations.
Note: FTAAPX includes all economies that are members of TPP, RCEP, and/or APEC.

Overlapping membership would also help to ensure that the initiatives do not devolve into competing regional blocs—the much-noted downside of regional FTAs. Countries involved in both negotiations are likely to align their provisions in order to simplify their internal policy adjustments. The similarity of the RCEP guidelines with the structure of the TPP has been noted already. Hopefully, the provisions within chapters will also generate similar text and institutional arrangements. This will not work in all cases, but a significant overlap will make it easier to consolidate the agreements in the future, or to advance shared provisions into future global negotiations.

The challenge to new members is that the TPP template is likely to be more rigorous and comprehensive than the RCEP template, and will, in part, reflect the interests of advanced countries (Petri and Plummer 2012). It will most likely include demanding provisions on services, intellectual property, and competition policy, as well as allowing fewer exceptions for sensitive sectors. Joining the TPP will require earlier and more difficult reforms than participation in the RCEP. At the same time, the benefits under the TPP template are estimated to be roughly twice as large as under the RCEP template, assuming they are applied to the same group of countries (say, in the context of the FTAAP). Moreover, the necessary reforms with ASEAN would in many cases parallel those required for full implementation of the AEC.

Implications for US Policy

As this study has argued, integration and the pursuit of centrality are likely to benefit ASEAN as well its principal partners, including the United States. The region's strategic and economic importance has been documented in earlier sections. This section examines how US policies *vis-à-vis* ASEAN have evolved, and recommends that they be further intensified, focusing on both selective integration with the region's most compatible economies and general support for the ASEAN project.

US Policies toward ASEAN

The United States has been engaged in Southeast Asia for a long time.[18] It was an early supporter of the Southeast Asia Treaty Organization

(SEATO), a security organization that preceded ASEAN, and it signed the Manila Pact of 1954, which remains in force as a collective defense treaty with Thailand and the Philippines. The United States became a dialogue partner of ASEAN in 1977, and has built up relations in fields ranging from security, economics, and trade to social and cultural affairs, as well as in development cooperation (Das 2013). But as the Cold War wound down, the United States turned its attention to trouble spots in Europe and the Middle East and to the rapid changes in Northeast Asia, leaving many observers with the feeling that its policies neglected Southeast Asia (Ba 2009).

The US should focus on selective integration with the region's most compatible economies and general support for the ASEAN project

These trends have been changing now for more than a decade. In 2002, the United States proposed an Enterprise for ASEAN Initiative (EAI), offering to negotiate bilateral Trade and Investment Framework Arrangements (TIFAs) and bilateral FTAs with countries willing to commit to reforms. The US-ASEAN TIFA was agreed upon in 2006, and a joint council was established to review cooperation projects. The United States concluded a bilateral FTA with Singapore in 2003, but negotiations with Thailand and Malaysia lingered under the EAI and were eventually overtaken by the TPP. In 2008, the United States appointed its first ambassador to ASEAN, a position converted two years later into a resident posting in Jakarta.

In modest ways, the United States has also supported the region's international economic strategy. In 2007, it launched the ASEAN Development Vision to Advance National Cooperation and Economic Integration (ADVANCE) project to support trade liberalization and facilitation in cooperation with the ASEAN Secretariat. ADVANCE has funded, for example, work on the ASEAN Single Window, which facilitates trade through electronic documentation. Despite these efforts, however, many in the region still felt that the US-ASEAN relationship was in a holding pattern, particularly in light of ever-deepening ASEAN relations with other dialogue partners.

Engagement is now clearly intensifying under President Barack Obama, who spent part of his childhood in Indonesia. In 2009, the

United States acceded to the Treaty of Amity and Cooperation in Southeast Asia (TAC), a long-standing ASEAN request, and participated in an ASEAN-US Leaders' Meeting in Singapore. It is true that US presidents have missed some key meetings in Asia—a result of the fact that participation requires several days of travel in the middle of what is typically a climactic period in US elections and budgetary politics—but the level of interest remains high.

In 2010, the United States joined the East Asia Summit (EAS) and became a member of the ASEAN Defense Ministers' Meeting Plus Eight (ADMM+8). In 2012, it participated in the first ASEAN-US business summit in Cambodia, and agreed to institutionalize an annual leaders' summit—in effect, committing the US president to meet with ASEAN leaders every year. The first such meeting launched the Expanded Economic Engagement (E3) initiative to facilitate the development of trade and investment flows.[19]

Unlike many other large countries, however, the United States has not sought to negotiate an FTA with ASEAN as a group. The region is thought to be too diverse to accept rigorous provisions, such as those now expected in the TPP.[20] Thus, the United States has dealt simultaneously with ASEAN as an institution in areas requiring less formal commitments, and with its individual member economies for forging deeper ties. As the next section argues, this policy makes sense and is consistent with the economics of maximizing gains from economic relations with the region.

A Framework for US-ASEAN Economic Relations

Despite the many connections between ASEAN and the United States documented in this study, there is no clear conceptual framework to guide interactions between the two economies. In fact, ASEAN centrality raises new challenges because it suggests collective policy positions that, in turn, are likely to favor least common denominator policies. These would make it possible, for example, for some member states to block disciplines that would be needed to deepen relations with the United States.

But economics suggests a solution—an approach that permits deep, selective ties, subject to the requirement that those ties also benefit third parties. In the ASEAN context, this prescription calls for deep FTAs with member countries prepared to meet those obligations, and parallel measures to strengthen relations with ASEAN as a whole, which would, in effect, compensate members that are not ready to participate in deep engagement. The theory itself says little about which parties should be involved in these compensating measures. However, most reasonably, both the benefiting ASEAN countries and the United States should help to extend the gains from deeper economic ties to the region as a whole.

The United States has, in fact, begun to follow such a two-speed approach. Conceptually, a policy that respects centrality and maximizes gains from ASEAN-US cooperation should:

- maximize cooperation with ASEAN members having the capacity for deep economic and investment relations with the United States;
- support ASEAN integration; and
- ensure, along with ASEAN partners, that new agreements involving some ASEAN countries would benefit all ASEAN members.

Such a strategy would preclude divide-and-conquer policies. It would champion deeper agreements with countries that are interested in them, but not threaten others with economic losses if they fail to participate. It calls for two kinds of US engagement with the region: (1) a deep track that promotes US agreements with countries that want to pursue further integration, and (2) a broad track that ensures support for ASEAN and benefits to all members.

> *A policy that respects centrality and maximizes gains from ASEAN-US cooperation would preclude divide-and-conquer policies*

The deep track includes formal trade agreements such as the TPP. Four member states are participating in the current negotiations, with Indonesia, the Philippines, and Thailand potentially joining them in the intermediate future. Simulations suggest that these countries would benefit substantially from membership. But the simulations also show tangible, although small, trade diversion *vis-à-vis* other ASEAN members. These side effects require compensation from the

United States (through the broad track discussed below) and from the ASEAN economies enjoying related benefits in order to engineer a Kemp-Wan outcome.

The broad track involves more varied and less formal support. So far, it has emphasized technological and other forms of cooperation and capacity building. Specific initiatives have included policy advice and capacity building for the ASEAN Secretariat, support for trade facilitation and the ASEAN Single Window, and guidance on regulatory reform. The United States has scaled up these efforts, and potential projects include other integration-related objectives, such as connectivity and infrastructure development, as well as educational and cultural initiatives. These policies provide a good fit for the region's less-developed members and reduce costs for international firms operating in regional markets.

An especially successful example is provided by US support for economic reform in Vietnam. After Vietnam launched its *doi moi* program and withdrew from Cambodia, the United States established diplomatic relations and, together with the World Bank, deepened its support for Vietnamese reform. Eventually, it concluded the US-Vietnam Bilateral Trade Agreement (BTA), which went into effect in December 2001. Although not an FTA per se, the BTA did address key issues that improved access to US markets and helped Vietnam prepare for accession to the WTO.[21] Throughout, the United States provided technical assistance through the "Support for Trade Acceleration" (STAR) project. The results speak for themselves: Vietnam was one of the poorest countries in the region in the 1990s, but reached middle-income status by 2012; trade to GDP at 155 percent is only second to Singapore in ASEAN; and the United States is Vietnam's second most important export market.

The availability of external integration options (such as the TPP) does not mean that every ASEAN member, even among those ready to do so, will need to participate in them. Most members will have good economic reasons to do so, and the benefit/cost ratios will rise further as the TPP expands to include more ASEAN and other members. However, for domestic or international political reasons, some ASEAN countries may decide not to pursue such ties. Indeed, recognizing the reality that these are fundamental, national decisions will minimize tensions within the region itself.

The two-speed approach provides an attractive way to structure engagement with selected countries, while promoting the interests of all ASEAN members. This is not just, or even predominantly, the responsibility of outside partners; it is a key ASEAN goal due to the value of integration to the region itself. To be sure, the calibration of the tracks will be challenging. The broad track should have sufficient resources committed to it so that its benefits offset the negative effects, both economic and political, on countries excluded from it.

Trade Policy

The Asia-Pacific region is again assuming center stage in US policy, in part due to the pivot/rebalancing strategy launched under former Secretary of State Hillary Clinton. More recently, Secretary of State John Kerry described a "Pacific Dream" of "unprecedented security, economic and social cooperation. We can break new ground in how we keep countries safe, help economies to mature, create new jobs, and embrace partnerships for the future. And we can do it while empowering people to make these choices for themselves" (Kerry 2013). Secretary Kerry emphasized the importance of "marketplaces that are fair, meaning that they are open, transparent, and accountable" and of the TPP itself.

While the Asia-Pacific economic community remains a centerpiece of America's Pacific Dream, US tactics have changed. They now emphasize a modern, high-quality trade agreement that the United States hopes to expand throughout the region and eventually beyond. As Secretary Kerry noted, ASEAN and its member states have to be on board for this project to work. To gain their participation, the

A cohesive Asia-Pacific economic community remains a centerpiece of America's 'Pacific Dream'

United States will have to reassure Southeast Asia that the TPP is not a challenge to ASEAN centrality, and it can telegraph this commitment by engaging all key ASEAN economies and offering vigorous support for ASEAN as a whole.

From the viewpoint of trade policy, this means, first, a broad strategy to help prepare all of the region's economies for participating successfully in high-quality international linkages. The E3 initiative is a promising vehicle for these efforts. It is a flexible approach that can be managed imaginatively. It should, most importantly, support ASEAN's efforts to realize the AEC and related integration objectives. It should also help to prepare individual ASEAN members for joining a high-quality regional trading system, such as the TPP. This requires identifying and supporting necessary reforms, including legal and regulatory changes within economies, and building capacity to make change possible.

Second, it argues for a deep strategy that brings more ASEAN economies into the TPP. The next three ASEAN economies likely to join the TPP are Indonesia, the Philippines, and Thailand. Regional integration and liberalization are mutually reinforcing and dynamic. With many ASEAN members already within the TPP or poised to join it, the region's own trade policies and regulatory systems are likely to drift toward higher international standards. And countries that are not yet members will see the value of membership rise as the first-round agreement is concluded and, perhaps, new partners will be attracted. It will become ever more costly for countries to stay out once, for example, South Korea, the Philippines, and others come on board.[22] Through informal negotiations, focused support through the E3, and steady efforts to publicize the potential benefits of open markets, progress can be made toward including all major ASEAN economies in the future TPP phases.

Third, an effective trade policy will make clear that the United States is not asking ASEAN to choose between Asian partners, including China, and the United States. Certainly, countries do not have to choose between RCEP and TPP. The RCEP will help to bring barriers down, and could contribute to building a better trading system that encompasses all Asian economies. This goal would also be well served by progress in China-US economic relations, as has been argued elsewhere (Petri and Plummer 2012). There are increasing indications at this writing that China is willing to consider deeper engagement with the United States and other TPP countries, perhaps through new negotiations that involve joining the TPP, an FTA with the United States, or, best of all, a path that leads to regionwide free trade.

The TPP itself can be designed to support these goals. It can include provisions that will be accessible to all reform-minded economies. It can focus those provisions on creating a level playing field to promote competition on the basis of economic efficiency, rather than adding rules that require specific governance or business systems. It can have an accession clause that makes it easy for new economies to join and, perhaps, identify future accession windows that make the process more predictable. Finally, the TPP could include an "umbrella" clause that would allow it to join forces with the RCEP, in case both trading systems emerge as important networks in the future. It is unlikely that all economies in the RCEP would join the TPP or vice versa, so bridging the two could become an attractive policy option. It is too early to focus on the details of such projects, but recognizing the possibility would help to ease concerns that countries are embarking on inconsistent tracks.

Complementary Policies

Trade policy initiatives can be reinforced by other initiatives to strengthen connections between ASEAN and the United States. In technology, education, and culture, the United States remains the most prominent partner of ASEAN economies and their citizens. Deeper political, economic, cultural, and scientific ties would be welcomed by the peoples of ASEAN and the American public, and initiatives could support efforts to enhance the visibility of the partnership.

The economic relationship between ASEAN and the United States remains strong, despite the fact that its statistics are not expanding as fast as those with other Asian countries, especially China. This trend is inevitable and should not affect the partnership negatively—economics is not a zero-sum game. Ideally, policymakers on both sides will understand that the absolute value of the relationship will grow, even if its relative size does not. ASEAN's relations with Asia and with the United States can both thrive. Much will depend on the foreign and economic policies of the United States itself, and on its relations with China. The good news, however, is that all these new, large partnerships would yield compelling economic benefits.

There is every reason to expect that ASEAN's relations with Asia and with the United States can both thrive

Conclusions

ASEAN is important to the United States for political and economic reasons, and its integration and continued economic growth will make it more so. Thus, the United States has a stake in sustaining ASEAN's development, and in promoting efforts to deepen the ASEAN-US relationship. At the same time, the United States and some ASEAN members also have interests that justify going beyond the regional relationships to deepen bilateral or plurilateral economic ties. Can these two objectives be pursued in parallel?

This paper provides an affirmative answer, based in part on economics, and in part on the favorable history of the ASEAN-US relationship. The United States has long supported ASEAN's development, with both security guarantees and economic and technical assistance. ASEAN integration and centrality serve US interests. US economic relations with the region are robust, and possibilities for still deeper ties are promising.

In an ideal world, the ASEAN-US relationship would intensify without concern for trade rules, which would be determined by a global system that keeps pace with the changing requirements of world trade. In practice, the task of drafting rules now mainly falls on regional arrangements. This is especially so in the Asia-Pacific region, where trade and investment are following unusually dynamic trajectories.

TPP and RCEP will both contribute to regional gains while producing positive spillovers for the world

The TPP and RCEP negotiations represent efforts to write such rules. These two negotiations, which some view as competitors, are, in fact, motivated by similar goals and both can help to create a new regionwide trading system with positive spillovers for the world. Nevertheless, they complicate the ASEAN-US relationship.

Several ASEAN economies have joined the TPP negotiations in order to achieve deeper integration through liberalization and new trade rules. But there are many critics of these developments who argue that the TPP could create divisions among ASEAN countries and impose trade and investment diversion losses on member states excluded from the TPP. However, restraining members from join-ing the TPP and foregoing significant economic gains would harm ASEAN's long-term interests and is not likely to succeed.

The solution to this dilemma is to follow two-speed policies. On one hand, the United States (like other important external partners) can engage countries that are ready for deeper ties by concluding agreements that maximize mutual benefits. On the other hand, the United States, working together with ASEAN as a unit, can also help to prepare other ASEAN countries for deeper engagement in the fu-ture. As this paper discussed, the dual approach has a solid economic pedigree based on the Kemp-Wan theorem. In practice, the approach calls for deeper integration through the TPP and stronger general relations with the region through policies that help to prepare it for global competition. The United States has generally pursued such an approach since it first concluded an FTA with Singapore in 2003 and adopted parallel initiatives to strengthen its ties with ASEAN as a whole. The right balance now calls for more vigorous action on the second of these tracks.

The pieces are in place to ratchet up both paths of engagement. The United States has proposed a new framework for lending sup-port through E3, focusing on trade facilitation and capacity building among low-income ASEAN members. It can use this framework to encourage high-quality trade agreements within Asia and to prepare all Asian members to enter the TPP eventually. These initiatives will also promote deeper integration within ASEAN itself, or—put an-other way—to strengthen the foundations of ASEAN centrality. At the same time, the United States should also offer an intensive coop-eration option through the TPP initiative. Four ASEAN members are now on board, and others should be encouraged to join as well.

This strategy provides a flexible approach for engaging ASEAN commensurate with its strategic significance. Implementing it ef-fectively will, of course, require leadership by the United States and ASEAN heads of state. An effective working relationship between China and the United States would greatly contribute to these efforts, since it would allow ASEAN to pursue economic objectives without concerns about having to choose between important partners. Close relations with ASEAN are essential, even given the other serious chal-lenges that the United States faces worldwide. ASEAN is central to, and may be a driver of, the development of the Asia-Pacific econo-my, a region that will arguably dominate the world economy in the decades ahead.

Appendix:
US-ASEAN Economic Prospects, 2010–2025

ASEAN's economic performance is strong; despite the global financial crisis, the region has grown at a 5.5 percent annual rate over the last six years. That momentum is expected to carry into the future, although growth rates will, of course, vary across countries with different levels of development and economic characteristics. This Appendix provides long-term projections of the ASEAN-US economic relationship based on simulations that incorporate external growth projections and the trade policy simulations reported in the text.

ASEAN is already a major US trade and investment partner. Many global supply chains, including those that ultimately end in US markets, pass through ASEAN. The region's global role is likely to increase with development, even as its connections turn toward other dynamic Asian economies. Over time, ASEAN-US relations will become more important to the United States, with ASEAN growing more than twice as fast as the US economy. The region will increasingly control manufacturing clusters that are currently located in other middle-income economies, such as China. Meanwhile, the United States will play an important, but slowly diminishing role in ASEAN's economic network.

ASEAN Economic Growth

The projections used in this study were developed by the French research institute CEPII (Foure et al. 2010) and are, in turn, based on UN projections of population growth and econometric projections of productivity growth and capital stock increases. Table A1 shows that ASEAN is expected to grow at a 6.2 percent annual rate between 2010 and 2025, a little faster than in recent years. To be sure, the CEPII projections were published in 2010 and, to some extent, reflect the high growth expectations of preceding years. From the perspective of 2013, for example, the growth rate projected for China (8.8 percent) seems a bit too high, but other rates, such as those for the Philippines (2.8 percent), predate the long-awaited acceleration of this economy and may be too low. No projection is likely to be accurate in all of its details, but the broad messages of the CEPII results continue to resonate with the region's favorable prospects.

CEPII forecasts especially rapid growth for the region's least developed economies (Cambodia, Lao PDR, Myanmar, and Vietnam) as they gain a foothold in global production chains, exploit ample supplies of labor, and pursue good opportunities for technological catch-up. The results also suggest fast growth in Indonesia, the largest of the region's economies, presumably reflecting the expectation that the country's reforms will continue to support solid investments and technological catch-up in the future. The projections envision deceleration in more advanced ASEAN economies (Malaysia, Thailand, and Singapore), due to a combination of aging populations, diminished opportunities for technological catch-up, and stiffer competition from China and other middle-income superpowers. Nevertheless, the results add up to healthy growth for the region as a whole, which is expected to increase its share of world GDP from 2.6 percent to 3.6 percent by 2025.

Meanwhile, advanced economies—the United States, Japan, and Europe—are expected to grow more slowly, at rates similar to those in the recent past. These projections indicate that income differentials between the advanced economies and Asia's emerging markets will continue to close; the ratio of per capita incomes in the United States to those in ASEAN is projected to fall from 17:1 in 2010 to 10:1 in 2025. As a result, the region's middle class (consisting of people with expenditures between $10 and $100 per person per day) will

Table A1. ASEAN Growth, 2010–2025							
	2010			2025			Growth Rate (%)
	Population (m)	GDP ($b)	GDP/cap ($)	Population (m)	GDP ($b)	GDP/cap ($)	
ASEAN	584.8	1,532	2,620	661.4	3,766	5,694	6.2
Brunei	0.4	11	27,277	0.5	19	38,767	3.8
Cambodia	14.1	12	826	14.1	38	2,688	8.2
Indonesia	232.6	550	2,367	262.2	1,549	5,909	6.3
Lao PDR	6.2	6	989	6.2	19	3,066	7.8
Malaysia	27.9	207	7,424	33.6	431	12,841	2.8
Myanmar	48.0	21	431	48.0	76	1,579	9.0
Philippines	93.9	163	1,734	116.6	322	2,757	2.8
Singapore	4.8	202	42,587	5.2	415	80,339	2.7
Thailand	68.3	266	3,896	71.5	558	7,803	3.8
Vietnam	88.7	94	1,060	103.6	340	3,281	7.1
United States	310.1	14,050	45,304	349.1	20,273	58,066	2.5
China	1340.7	4,850	3,617	1425.7	17,249	12,099	8.8
Japan	127.5	4,250	33,332	120.4	5,338	44,319	1.5
Europe	499.9	16,629	33,265	501.4	22,714	45,305	2.1
Others	3994.4	17,133	4,289	4866.6	33,882	6,962	4.7
World	6857.5	58,445	8,523	7924.7	103,223	13,025	3.9

Source: Authors' simulations.

grow from 24 percent to 50 percent of the population (Petri and Zhai 2013). Thus, ASEAN will become an increasingly attractive market to US producers and a desirable partner for US policymakers.

Trade and Investment

Given ASEAN's solid economic record, it is not surprising that the region is a leading trade and investment partner of the United States. Its trade and investment positions are summarized in Table A2. Taken together, the ASEAN economies account for about 5 percent of US

Table A2. ASEAN-US Trade and Investment, 2010–2025

	ASEAN	Indonesia	Malaysia	Philippines	Singapore	Thailand	Vietnam	Others
US exports to partner								
Value 2010 ($mill)	81,484	10,161	12,600	9,809	30,486	14,054	3,674	699
% of US exports	5.3	0.7	0.8	0.6	2.0	0.9	0.2	0.0
% of partner imports	9.5	6.6	8.1	11.8	16.1	7.7	5.0	4.1
Value 2025 ($mill)	152,303	28,675	21,456	15,954	38,939	35,711	9,714	1,854
% of US exports	5.4	1.0	0.8	0.6	1.4	1.3	0.3	0.1
% of partner imports	7.9	6.2	7.1	9.6	14.2	7.9	4.3	4.3
US imports from partner								
Value 2010 ($mill)	152,981	25,306	36,281	14,699	27,260	28,755	17,146	3,533
% of US imports	7.2	1.2	1.7	0.7	1.3	1.4	0.8	0.2
% of partner exports	16.3	12.5	17.4	13.8	10.8	12.7	19.5	14.2
Value 2025 ($mill)	226,720	49,704	35,747	21,617	17,451	43,992	50,239	7,969
% of US imports	6.6	1.5	1.0	0.6	0.5	1.3	1.5	0.2
% of partner exports	11.2	8.3	8.6	9.9	4.8	7.8	17.5	12.4
US FDI stock in partner								
Value 2010 ($mill)	142,969	14,271	16,228	4,610	95,587	11,635	605	33

Table A2. ASEAN-US Trade and Investment, 2010–2025 (continued)

	ASEAN	Indonesia	Malaysia	Philippines	Singapore	Thailand	Vietnam	Others
% of US outward FDI	4.1	0.4	0.5	0.1	2.8	0.3	0.0	0.0
% of partner inward FDI	16.4	10.2	19.1	16.7	21.0	9.1	2.8	0.3
Value 2025 ($mill)	452,316	61,066	53,824	13,395	284,597	36,549	2,795	89
% of US outward FDI	5.2	0.7	0.6	0.2	3.3	0.4	0.0	0.0
% of partner inward FDI	13.6	8.4	17.5	16.2	18.2	7.7	2.4	0.1
Partner FDI stock in US								
Value 2010 ($mill)	22,957	143	509	159	21,116	1,018	12	0
% of US inward FDI	1.0	0.0	0.0	0.0	0.9	0.0	0.0	0.0
% of partner outward FDI	5.3	2.6	0.7	2.5	7.8	4.3	2.1	0.0
Value 2025 ($mill)	68,885	612	1,689	461	62,868	3,199	56	0
% of US inward FDI	1.4	0.0	0.0	0.0	1.3	0.1	0.0	0.0
% of partner outward FDI	3.1	1.4	0.4	1.5	4.7	2.2	1.5	0.0

Source: Model data and projections (Petri et al. 2012b)
Note: Values are given in f.o.b. terms in 2007 US dollars. 2010 values may differ slightly from actual data since they are projected using the model from its 2007 base year data.

exports and 7 percent of US imports (roughly twice their share of world GDP), ranking fourth among US trade partners—below China, Canada, and Mexico, but above Japan, Germany, and the United Kingdom. Except for China, they are also growing more rapidly than other top US partners. ASEAN plays a slightly less prominent role in investment, accounting for about 5 percent of US total two-way FDI. But it is still one of the top dozen or so US partners.

Five economies—the original ASEAN-5: Indonesia, Malaysia, the Philippines, Singapore, and Thailand—account for most of these transactions, with Singapore, despite its small population, being the most important among them. Singapore absorbs 37 percent of US exports and 92 percent of US FDI to ASEAN. These five economies, plus Vietnam, play roughly equal roles in US imports from the region. Our projections suggest, however, that US transactions with Malaysia and Singapore will grow less rapidly than those with other ASEAN economies, partly because these two countries run large trade surpluses that are assumed to moderate in the future. By 2025, Indonesia and Thailand will be nearly as important destinations for US exports as Singapore, although in terms of inward FDI flows, they will continue to trail Singapore by a large margin. Overall, US transactions with ASEAN will become more diversified across countries. While not included in the projections, the removal of sanctions on Myanmar, a country that has great potential and has previously contributed significantly to the region's economy, will further enhance the importance and diversification of ASEAN.

As a whole, ASEAN will become more important to the external transactions of the United States by 2025 than it is today, but not dramatically so. ASEAN's share of US exports will increase slightly, and its share of US FDI markedly, from 4 percent in 2010 to 5 percent in 2025. FDI from ASEAN to the United States will also grow, rising from 1.0 percent in 2010 to 1.4 percent. But imports from ASEAN will decline from 7.2 percent to 6.6 percent of total US imports, a result of pressure from other Asian exporters, including China. Meanwhile, ASEAN's exports will shift toward rapidly growing Asian partners. From ASEAN's viewpoint, trade and investment relations with the United States will diminish relative to total external transactions. But the United States will remain a very important partner, especially for exports and FDI inflows.

Sectoral Structure of the Trade Relationship

The structure of ASEAN-US trade in 2010 is presented in Tables A3 (US exports) and A4 (US imports). Trade was imbalanced, with US imports from ASEAN roughly double the size of US exports. This was a reflection of the large overall US trade deficit, as well as ASEAN's large surpluses, led by Malaysia and Singapore. Both directions of flows were dominated by manufactures, but while US manufactures imports exceeded manufactures exports by around 2.5:1, the trade balance was reversed in services, with US exports exceeding US imports by a nearly 2:1 margin.

US manufactured exports went, to a large extent, to Singapore, with chemicals, electrical equipment, machinery, and transport equipment (including airplanes) dominating the mix. Other important manufacturing exports by the United States included electrical equipment to Malaysia and the Philippines, two additional electronic manufacturing centers of the region. US manufacturing exports to Thailand were more evenly distributed across several sectors.

US manufactured imports were more distinctly specialized, following the patterns of comparative advantage of individual countries. Electrical equipment came primarily from Malaysia, Thailand, and Singapore, while textiles and apparel came from Indonesia and Vietnam. Chemical, machinery, and other manufactures were more evenly distributed.

US service trade was dominated by the exports of private business services to essentially all ASEAN economies, and by trade, transport, communications, and private service imports from Thailand and Singapore.

The challenge for US trade with ASEAN is that today's principal markets—Malaysia and Singapore—will grow less rapidly than the rest of the region. Nevertheless, both countries' imports will grow relatively quickly, as their trade surpluses shrink to yield more balanced external capital positions.

Looking ahead, the United States can expect brisk growth in its trade with ASEAN (Table A5). The growth will reflect the relatively fast expansion of ASEAN economies, and the narrowing trade surpluses of those with large current imbalances (particularly Malaysia and Singapore). The trade balance between ASEAN and the United States will remain nearly constant at around $70 billion, but since

Table A3. US Exports to ASEAN, 2010 ($bill)

	ASEAN	Indonesia	Malaysia	Philippines	Singapore	Thailand	Vietnam	Others
Primary products	**4,253**	**1,950**	**446**	**467**	**782**	**153**	**443**	**12**
Rice	6	1	1	0	0	4	0	1
Wheat	853	289	45	334	118	25	41	0
Other agriculture	3,136	1,562	373	124	581	100	386	9
Mining	259	99	27	9	83	24	15	2
Manufactures	**55,765**	**5,016**	**9,033**	**8,236**	**8,903**	**22,292**	**1,945**	**339**
Food, beverages	3,683	943	528	919	542	324	403	25
Textiles	572	176	39	30	200	55	67	4
Apparel, footwear	352	26	24	19	98	57	123	4
Chemicals	8,553	1,098	935	498	1,996	3,648	348	30
Metals	2,807	288	647	140	559	1,029	137	6
Electrical equipment	15,037	182	4,269	5,156	2,000	3,306	112	11
Machinery	12,361	942	1,666	920	1,623	6,877	278	55
Transport equipment	9,832	992	616	159	1,189	6,416	282	179
Other manufactures	2,568	369	308	396	696	579	196	25

Table A3. US Exports to ASEAN, 2010 ($bill) (continued)

	ASEAN	Indonesia	Malaysia	Philippines	Singapore	Thailand	Vietnam	Others
Services	21,465	3,195	3,121	1,105	4,369	8,041	1,286	349
Utilities	144	5	3	2	26	105	1	2
Construction	278	93	39	8	40	65	25	8
Trade, transport, comm.	5,231	359	462	291	948	2,774	322	74
Private services	12,428	2,120	2,128	643	2,574	4,207	582	174
Public services	3,384	617	489	161	782	891	355	90
Total	81,484	10,161	12,600	9,809	14,054	30,486	3,674	699

Source: Authors' simulations.
Note: Values are in 2007 US dollars expressed in f.o.b. terms.

Table A4. US Imports from ASEAN, 2010 ($bill)

	ASEAN	Indonesia	Malaysia	Philippines	Singapore	Thailand	Vietnam	Others
Primary products	**2,137**	**304**	**68**	**64**	**404**	**9**	**1,177**	**111**
Rice	232	3	3	2	219	0	3	2
Wheat	0	0	0	0	0	0	0	0
Other agriculture	961	223	30	62	168	8	463	8
Mining	944	78	35	0	18	0	712	102
Manufactures	**140,026**	**23,876**	**34,730**	**14,093**	**26,019**	**22,602**	**15,603**	**3,102**
Food, beverages	4,023	486	737	555	1,645	84	507	8
Textiles	**6,397**	**2,155**	**244**	**317**	**570**	**61**	**2,063**	**986**
Apparel, footwear	21,573	6,338	635	2,098	1,530	65	8,880	2,026
Chemicals	15,971	4,915	2,155	287	3,110	5,185	288	30
Metals	3,689	921	614	271	1,371	177	330	5
Electrical equipment	53,260	2,058	22,472	7,013	10,640	10,759	315	3
Machinery	20,602	2,386	5,537	2,646	3,967	5,361	698	8
Transport equipment	2,275	283	231	339	696	659	55	11
Other manufactures	12,237	4,334	2,104	567	2,491	250	2,466	24

Table A4. US Imports from ASEAN, 2010 ($bill) (continued)

	ASEAN	Indonesia	Malaysia	Philippines	Singapore	Thailand	Vietnam	Others
Services	**10,817**	1,126	1,483	542	2,332	4,650	366	319
Utilities	16	4	8	0	2	1	0	1
Construction	80	22	12	3	12	20	6	4
Trade, transport, comm.	5,360	578	777	365	1,756	1,629	113	142
Private services	4,914	407	623	163	541	2,843	205	132
Public services	447	114	63	12	20	157	42	39
Total	**152,981**	**25,306**	**36,281**	**14,699**	**28,755**	**27,260**	**17,146**	**3,533**

Source: Authors' simulations.
Note: Values are in 2007 US dollars expressed in f.o.b. terms.

Table A5. Projected Growth of ASEAN-US Trade by Sector, 2010–2025

	ASEAN	Indonesia	Malaysia	Philippines	Singapore	Thailand	Vietnam	Others
US exports to partner	**4.3**	**7.2**	**3.6**	**3.3**	**6.4**	**1.6**	**6.7**	**6.7**
Primary products	5.9	6.8	3.6	1.3	4.8	3.2	8.8	6.5
Manufactures	2.1	5.5	2.0	2.5	3.2	0.0	4.7	2.1
Services	7.8	9.3	7.0	8.0	10.6	4.9	8.3	9.5
US imports from partner	**2.7**	**4.6**	**-0.1**	**2.6**	**2.9**	**-2.9**	**7.4**	**5.6**
Primary products	-1.6	-2.4	1.0	5.3	0.2	-1.9	-3.0	-1.5
Manufactures	2.8	4.6	-0.1	2.6	2.9	-3.4	7.9	6.1
Services	1.5	5.0	0.3	3.0	3.1	-0.9	3.6	0.6

Source: Authors' simulations.

trade will grow, this means that the United States will experience much higher growth rates for its relatively low exports than for its relatively high imports.

Not surprisingly, the fastest growing export and import partners are likely to be economies that are themselves growing fast—Indonesia, Vietnam, and other ASEAN economies (Cambodia, Lao PDR, and Myanmar). Yet exports to all other economies will also grow. Services will be the fastest growing US export sector, although growth rates should be solid also in primary products and manufacturing.

US exports will grow nearly twice as fast as US imports, with imports from Malaysia and Singapore declining. However, imports from the region's less developed countries—Vietnam, Indonesia, and others—will continue to expand, as these countries establish manufacturing clusters that take over the production of some labor-intensive products from China. Meanwhile, ASEAN's primary goods exports to the US will decline, as the region makes more intensive use of its own resources, urbanization intensifies, and production shifts toward higher value-added manufacturing and services.

Endnotes

1. The proceedings of a recent ASEAN-US dialogue provide an interesting overview of this and other viewpoints from the perspectives of ASEAN and US speakers (Heng 2012).

2. A concise summary of ASEAN concerns about the effects of external trade agreements on centrality is provided by Kassim 2012.

3. Given the trade policy context, this paper focuses on real (as opposed to financial) relationships between ASEAN and the United States, especially production and trade. Other issues arise in the context of ASEAN's relationships with regional and global financial markets, but since these involve different, complex institutions, they are not addressed in this study.

4. The data in this paragraph are from the United Nations Commodity Trade Statistics Database (UN Comtrade).

5. IMF Trade Direction Database.

6. Cambodia was slated to join in 1997, along with Lao PDR and Myanmar, but it underwent a political coup that year and, hence, didn't formally join until two years later.

7. See http://aseanregionalforum.asean.org/about.html. Members include the 10 ASEAN countries, plus Timor-Leste, Papua New Guinea, China, Japan, Mongolia, North Korea, South Korea, Bangladesh, India, Pakistan, Sri Lanka, Australia, New Zealand, Canada, the EU, Russia, and the United States.

8. A good example is provided by the operation of WTO rules and the related dispute resolution mechanism in recent years. Despite the intense political pressures generated by the Great Recession, countries have generally refrained from overt protectionist responses, turning instead to WTO cases to address internal political pressures.

9. See, for example, Das 2013 for a recent assessment of progress thus far and remaining challenges.

10. Chia and Plummer (Cambridge University Press, forthcoming).

11. See http://www.aseanbriefing.com/news/2013/04/26/asean-summit-in-brunei-aec -and-the-southchina-sea.html.

12. Chairman's statement, http://www.asean.org/news/asean-statement-communiques /item/chairmansstatement-of-the-22nd-asean-summit-our-people-our-future- together.

13. See www.aric.adb.org, accessed July 18, 2013.

14. Cambodia, Lao PDR, and Myanmar are not APEC members.

15. India is also unconnected to these three countries, but its economic integration with Northeast Asia is far less significant (and the political dimension much less complicated).

16. The results in Table 5 and those in Table 4 on ASEAN's internal integration efforts were generated in different studies by slightly different models, and ask somewhat different questions. Nevertheless, estimates for comparable scenarios are similar. For example, Table 4 shows that moving from the AEC to the AEC+ would increase ASEAN incomes by 3.5 percent. A similar scenario in Table 5 involves moving from the baseline (which includes the AEC) to the RCEP, which is similar to AEC+ although not fully comparable, since the RCEP also includes FTAs among China, India, Japan, and South Korea (CIJK). Under the RCEP, ASEAN benefits are estimated as 2.1 percent of income. This estimate is appropriately smaller than under AEC+, since preferential access among the large Asian economies would erode ASEAN advantage. Similar comparisons are possible between the AEC++ and FTAAPX scenarios, showing incomes rising by 6.3 percent in Table 4 and 6.2 percent in Table 5 compared to a baseline that includes the AEC.

17. Tables 5 and 6 assume full employment of labor, as is typical of CGE modeling. This is a reasonable assumption given the long-run nature of these models. However, including the possibility of unemployed labor prior to integration potentially increases significantly the impact of economic integration by drawing in untapped factors of production. For example, Plummer et al. (forthcoming) estimates the effects of the AEC and RCEP on labor markets in six ASEAN economies, including three categories of skilled labor, three categories of semi-skilled labor, and unskilled labor. While the estimates are not directly comparable to those in Tables 5 and 6 given differences in parametric assumptions—e.g., with respect to changes in trade costs and the extent of NTB liberalization—the simulations in that paper show large gains in semi-skilled and unskilled jobs and wages, as well as far greater increases in income growth than in either Petri et al. (2012a) or this paper (i.e., increases in aggregate income of 8.3 percent and 18.9 percent for the AEC and RCEP, respectively).

18. For an overview, see Lum, Dolven, Manyin, Martin, and Vaughn 2009.

19. The White House, Office of the Press Secretary, "Fact Sheet: The US-ASEAN Expanded Economic Engagement (E3) Initiative," November 19, 2012.

20. The EAI was designed to be an umbrella for bilateral FTAs with individual ASEAN economies based on the Singapore-US FTA. Under this arrangement, the United States entered into bilateral FTA negotiations with Thailand and Malaysia, but neither resulted in a deal. For details on the economics of the EAI, see Naya and Plummer 2006.

21. For details regarding the BTA, see http://vietnam.usembassy.gov/econ12.html.

22. South Korea is the most promising candidate in the short term. In December 2013, on the sidelines of the WTO Ninth Ministerial Meeting in Bali, it began to launch preliminary bilateral talks with TPP negotiating partners in anticipation of possibly joining.

Bibliography

ASEAN. 2007. *ASEAN Economic Community Blueprint.* Jakarta: ASEAN Secretariat.

———. 2009. *Roadmap for an ASEAN Community 2009–2015.* Jakarta: ASEAN Secretariat.

———. 2012. "Guiding Principles and Objectives for Negotiating the Regional Comprehensive Economic Partnership," adopted by ASEAN ministers on August 30 in Siem Reap, Cambodia.

Asian Development Bank. 2013. *Asian Economic Integration Monitor.* Manila: Asian Development Bank.

Atje, Raymond. 2008. "ASEAN Economic Community: In Search of a Coherent External Policy." In Soesastro, Hadi, ed. 2008. *Deepening Economic Integration: The ASEAN Economic Community and Beyond.* ERIA Research Project Report 2007-1-2. Chiba, Japan: IDE-JETRO (Institute of Developing Economies).

Ba, Alice. 2009. "Systemic Neglect? A Reconsideration of US-Southeast Asia Policy." *Contemporary Southeast Asia 31*(3): 369–398.

Das, Sanchita Basu. 2013. "The Next Decade in ASEAN-USA Economic Relations." *ISEAS Perspective,* Institute of Southeast Asian Studies, Singapore, March 11.

Deunden, Nikomborirak, 2012. "An Assessment of the Implementation of AEC Service Liberalisation Milestones," Paper presented at the ASEAN Roundtable 2012 on Examining the ASEAN Economic Community Scorecard. ISEAS. May 2012.

Fitriani, Evi. 2010. "ASEAN and Contemporary US Diplomacy in East Asia." *Jakarta Post,* August 13.

Fouré, Jean, Agnès Bénassy-Quéré, and Lionel Fontagné. 2010. *The World Economy in 2050: A Tentative Picture.* Paris: CEPII (Centre d'Etudes Prospectives et d'Informations Internationales).

Heng, Pek Koon. 2012. *US-ASEAN-EAS Strategic Dialogue Symposium Overview Report.* Washington, DC: American University ASEAN Studies Center.

Hiratsuka, Daisuke, Ikumo Isono, Hitoshi Sato, and So Umezaki. 2008. "Escaping from FTA Trap and Spaghetti Bowl Problem in East Asia: An Insight from the Enterprise Survey in Japan." In Soesastro, Hadi, ed. 2008. *Deepening Economic Integration.* Chiba: IDE-JETRO

Humaidah, Ida. 2012. *Questioning ASEAN Centrality in East Asian Regionalism: The Case of ASEAN Connectivity.* Master's thesis, International Institute of Social Studies, Erasmus University, Rotterdam, the Netherlands.

Johnston, Alastair Iain. 2003. "Socialization in International Institutions: The ASEAN Way and International Relations Theory." In Ikenberry, G. John, and Michael Mastanduno, eds. 2003. *International Relations Theory of the Asia-Pacific.* New York: Columbia University Press.

Jones, Lee. 2010. "Still in the 'Driver's Seat,' But for How Long? ASEAN's Capacity for Leadership in East-Asian International Relations." *Journal of Current Southeast Asian Affairs* 29(3): 95–113.

Kassim, Yang Razali. 2012. "East Asia Summit 2012: Power Game in Asia Unfolds," *East Asia Forum,* December 12. http://www.eastasiaforum.org/2012/12/12/east-asia-summit-2012-asiaspower-game-unfolds/.

Kawai, Masahiro and Ganeshan Wignaraja, 2011. *Asia's Free Trade Agreements: How Is Business Responding?* (Cheltenham: ADB, ADBI, Edward Elgar). Available at: http://www.adbi.org/files/2011.01.31.book.asia.free.trade.agreements.pdf

Kemp, Murray C., and Henry Y. Wan. 1976. "An Elementary Proposition Concerning the Formation of Customs Unions." *Journal of International Economics* 6: 95–98.

Kerry, John. 2013. "Remarks on a 21st Century Pacific Partnership," US Department of State website. Retrieved April 15, http://www.state.gov/secretary/remarks/2013/04/207487.htm.

Lipsey, R.G. 1960. "The Theory of Customs Unions: A General Survey." *The Economic Journal* 70(279): 496–513. Retrieved from http://www.jstor.org/stable/10.2307/2228805.

Liu Zhun. 2013. "TPP May Spur China's Laggardly Reforms," *Global Times,* Beijing, May 6.

Lum, Thomas, Ben Dolven, Mark E. Manyin, Michael F. Martin, and Bruce Vaughn. 2009. *United States Relations with the Association of Southeast Asian Nations (ASEAN).* Report R40933. Washington, DC: Congressional Research Service of the Library of Congress, November 16.

Naya, Seiji, and Michael G. Plummer. 1991. "ASEAN Economic Cooperation in the New International Economic Environment." *ASEAN Economic Bulletin* 7(3): 261–276.

———. 2006. "A Quantitative Survey of the Economics of ASEAN-US Free Trade Agreements." *ASEAN Economic Bulletin* 23(2): 230–252. Retrieved from http://muse.jhu.edu/journals/ase/summary/v023/23.2naya.html.

Petri, Peter A. 2009. "Competitiveness and Leverage." In Plummer, Michael G., and Chia Siow Yue, eds. 2009. *Realizing the ASEAN Economic Community: A Comprehensive Assessment.* Singpore: Institute of Southeast Asian Studies Press.

Petri, Peter A., and Michael G. Plummer. 2012. *The Trans-Pacific Partnership and Asia-Pacific Integration: Policy Implications*. Peterson Institute for International Economics Policy Brief PB12-16. Retrieved from http://papers.ssrn.com/sol3/papers.cfm?abstract_id=2108399.

Petri, Peter A., Michael G. Plummer, and Fan Zhai. 2012a. "ASEAN Economic Community: A General Equilibrium Analysis." *Asian Economic Journal* 26(2): 93–118.

———. 2012b. *The Trans-Pacific Partnership and Asia-Pacific Integration: A Quantitative Assessment*. Washington, DC: Peterson Institute for International Economics.

Petri, Peter A., and Tri Thanh Vo. 2012. "Asian and Trans-Pacific Initiatives in Regional Integration". In *State of the Region 2012–2013*. Singapore: Pacific Economic Cooperation Council. Retrieved from http://papers.ssrn.com/sol3/papers.cfm?abstract_id=2148790.

Petri, Peter A., and Fan Zhai. 2013. "Navigating a Changing World Economy: ASEAN, the People's Republic of China, and India," Asian Development Bank Institute Working Paper, no. 404.

Pitsuwan, Surin. 2009. "Building an ASEAN Economic Community in the Heart of East Asia," keynote speech delivered at the East Asia Beyond the Global Economic Crisis international symposium, Tokyo, December.

Plummer, Michael G., and Chia Siow Yue, eds. 2009. *Realizing the ASEAN Economic Community: A Comprehensive Assessment*. Singapore: Institute of Southeast Asian Studies Press.

Plummer, Michael G., Peter A. Petri, and Fan Zhai. Forthcoming. "Assessing the Impacts of ASEAN Economic Integration on Labour Markets," Thematic Study prepared for ILO/ADB, ASEAN Community 2015: Managing Prosperity for Shared Prosperity and Social Progress.

Ravenhill, John. 2009. "East Asian Regionalism: Much Ado about Nothing?" *Review of International Studies* 35:215–235. Retrieved from http://journals.cambridge.org/production/action/cjoGetFulltext?fulltextid=5078628.

Thompson, Eric C. and Chulanee Thianthai. 2008. *Attitudes and Awareness toward ASEAN: Findings of a Ten Nation Survey*. Singapore: Institute of Southeast Asian Studies.

Viner, Jacob. 1950. *The Customs Union Issue*. New York: Carnegie Endowment for International Peace.

Zhai, Fan. 2008. "Armington Meets Melitz: Introducing Firm Heterogeneity in a Global CGE Model of Trade. *Journal of Economic Integration* 23(3): 575–604.

Acknowledgments

The quantitative analysis in this issue of Policy Studies draws extensively on results obtained through a long-standing collaboration between the authors and Fan Zhai, managing director of the China Investment Corporation. The authors also wish to thank Tim Buehrer, Giovanni Cappanelli, Chia Siow Yue, Dieter Ernst, Satu Limaye, Jayant Menon, Charles E. Morrison, Marcus Noland, Tri Thanh Vo and James Wallar for comments on a previous draft. We also thank Khalid Umar for excellent research assistance.

www.ingramcontent.com/pod-product-compliance
Lightning Source LLC
Chambersburg PA
CBHW050552280326
41933CB00011B/1812